Tales
of the
Jersey Devil

Tales
of the
Jersey Devil

by Geoffrey Girard

Middle Atlantic Press

Manufactured in the United States

1 2 3 4 5   08 07 06 05 04

Library of Congress Cataloging-in-Publication Data

Girard, Geoffrey.

Tales of the Jersey Devil / by Geoffrey Girard.

p. cm.

ISBN 0-9754419-2-2

1. Tales--New Jersey. 2. Devil. I. Title.

GR110.N2G57 2004

398.2'09749'01--dc22

2004025966

Cover design: Vicki Manucci and Terence Doherty

Interior design and composition: Vicki Manucci

Illustrations by Jared Barber

For information write:

Middle Atlantic Press

10 Twosome Drive

Moorestown, NJ 08057

For Gertrude Girard (G.G.)

Who introduced me to ghosts, witches and spells, and all those other fun things

that go bump in the night. And who always liked a good scary story.

ACKNOWLEDGMENTS

Thank you to the New Jersey State Police Department (specifically Kevin and Jack), the Camden County Historical Society, Yahoo's 18th Century Midwife Club (specifically British Annie), the New Jersey Division of Parks and Forestry, the village of Smithville, Father Lane, McLaughlin Photography in West Chester, the gifted Jared Barber, and to the whole gang at the Jersey Devil Club. Thank you to Mr. Harry Leeds for his remarkable generosity of time, support, and information.

Thanks to Mary, Erich, and Doug for reading or listening to all the first drafts and subsequently knowing more about the Jersey Devil than anyone from Ohio really should. An extra nod to Erich for riding shotgun on one of the Jersey fieldtrips to find the big JD. (Doug, we promise to take you next time.) To Terence Doherty and Middle Atlantic Press for your noteworthy collaboration and confidence. To friends who supported the process and encouraged in many ways throughout. To Mom, for extra research, editing, and coercing Dad into excessive fieldwork.

To Father, Dr. Jolyon P. Girard, for agreeing to join this curious project and its sizeable research. Your experience and excellence as a history professor and published historian, were key to the book's initiation and development. Your support and love as a father, even more so.

Special gratitude to James McCloy and Ray Miller, Jr. for their seminal research and publication, *The Jersey Devil* (Middle Atlantic Press) and introducing a certain nine-year-old to the Leeds Devil in 1976. That little red book, and the wonders within, have been part of this author's library and imagination for almost thirty years, and this book would not have been possible without.

CONTENTS

INTRODUCTION 11

BIRTH DAY 1735 13

LIVING IN DARKNESS 1738 22

LEGION 1740 32

CAPTAIN DECATUR AND THE WIZARD 1809 . . .42

UNDERGROUND 1858 53

DEADLINES 1909 .64

CAUGHT! 1913 73

GHOSTS 1954 82

INTO THE ABYSS 1969 93

BIRDS OF A FEATHER 1978 103

FRIGHT NIGHT 1986 114

THE JERSEY DEVIL CLUB 2004 124

THE WITCH'S CURSE 1735 134

INTRODUCTION

The tales you're about to read are based on the Jersey Devil myth, an American legend shared on dark nights for almost three hundred years. Many believe that the monster is more than myth; that it is an actual creature like the Northwest's Big Foot or Scotland's Loch Ness Monster; and that it still roams the woods daring to be found. Whichever case proves true, those new to the Jersey Devil are always surprised to learn I'm not just making this stuff up. Each story is a dramatization of the creature's known behaviors and history.

As with all oral folklore, variations appear throughout the myth. For these stories, I have used the most popular accounts of the tale and made notes at the end of each chapter where alternative versions warrant note.

New Jersey is not just turnpikes, factories, and malls. If you think that, you've never spent any time there. There are hundreds of miles of Atlantic coastline, and one fifth of the state, one million acres, remains covered in an undeveloped forest called the Pine Barrens. Smack in between New York City and Philadelphia, within the most densely populated state in the country, is an ancient and mostly deserted forest the size of Delaware. This is where the Jersey Devil lives.

BIRTH DAY
1735

Despite the violent thunder storm raging around them, the midwife was slow to follow the boy into the house. She hovered just outside the opened doorway and the cold biting rain and howling winds that had swept suddenly across the Pine Barrens beat past her cloaked form into the Leeds home. The promising warmth of a fire within briefly touched her chilled face as she carefully studied the many shadows dancing against the bare walls of the candlelit cottage. The other children milled about the front room, waiting for the birthing.

Lightening burst again just behind the house. The Barrens blushed suddenly in blue radiance, the glow trickling through endless walls of pine. The midwife turned to the drenched girl shivering in the darkness beside her. "You can still leave now," she offered over the driving rain and accompanying after-rumble of thunder.

The girl looked up at her, the rain pelting her hooded face. She knew the house they were about to enter, the baby she was to help deliver. She, too, had heard the whispers from the other women. Dark gossip. Cursed by a gypsy woman, some said. Others went so far as to suggest that Leeds herself had dabbled in the *darker arts* . . . in witchcraft. A thirteenth child cursed and shaped for Lucifer himself. The Leeds baby.

"Come on, then," the boy beckoned urgently, returning to the doorway. "It's comin'!"

The girl shook off the rain and stepped boldly past the midwife into the house.

She found a roomful of children within. Five boys, including the one they'd followed, and five girls ranging in ages from three to sixteen. The younger children sat in a small circle in front of the fire. The older siblings stood frozen in various spots about the room. Each eyed the two strangers sternly, both defensive and proud.

One of the girls took her wet cloak and Mary shook the storm out of her hair. The rain battered the roof above with a fury she found now somehow louder and more frightening than the storm she'd raced through outside.

"Took you an infernal time," the oldest boy snapped. It was unclear if he'd directed the barb at his own soaked brother. "Who's she?" he pointed.

"'Tis my apprentice," the midwife replied, rubbing her hands to warm them.

"You be Clement Hillman's girl, ain't that so?" the boy said, leaning in close. His breath reeked of applejack, the force of the crude alcohol even more evident in his bullying eyes. He looked quite a bit like his father, who'd left the family for good several months before.

"I am by God's blessing," the girl replied carefully. "Mary Hillman." Groans of labor suddenly spilled from the room just beyond.

"Well, Mary Hillman," he drawled, tapping his chest. "I suspect you better get this foul night ended."

The midwife nodded and nudged Mary to follow her as one of the girls held the dark curtain aside for the two to enter the bedroom. Mother Leeds lay on her side, her two eldest daughters hovering around the bed. Several candles flickered on a short table beside them, casting dark shadows throughout the room. Mary felt as if the very Barrens had somehow crept into the house, something dim and sinister.

"It's not moving down," one of the daughters mumbled. Her face was pale and gaunt, her eyes filled with dread. "We tried to do it ourselves but . . . but Mama's gone so painful. We didn't know what else to do."

"Bless your soul, you done just fine, darling." The midwife nodded. "You were right keen to send for me." The girl smiled just enough. "But we've gotta get her up and into a squat to help the baby move down," the midwife explained out loud, mostly to Mary. It was only the girl's second delivery. And the first, she'd been out getting more cloths when the baby had finally come.

"Go away," the Leeds women muttered from the bed. "Just let us be." She scowled suddenly, the contraction clearly hitting fast and hard. Thunder cracked again just overhead.

"Mary," the midwife continued, "You and the girls find some rags and get this cleaned up. Need another sheet and see to filling the water pitcher. Quick to it now." She swept over to the bed. "Come, Hannah," she said and leaned in close to the Leeds women. "You gotta get up."

"Leave now," Mother Leeds said again. "Or . . ." She glared at them, her voice turning to a snarl. "Or do you want to birth the devil?"

Mary watched as the midwife firmly grabbed hold of Hannah Leeds's face and leaned in close to make sure the two older women were eye-to-eye. "That'll be enough," she warned. "God's breath and blessing, there'll be no more of . . . of that, tonight."

Mother Leeds stared into the midwife's face for a long while before turning her head away. "I feel my baby moving," she cried suddenly.

"Yes," the midwife smiled. "Of course you do. Lord care for us all. Now grab hold and I'll help you up." Mother Leeds sighed and wrapped her arms around the midwife, shaking with another contraction.

Mary followed the girls to another room and collected everything asked for. Over the rain and thunder, she heard Leeds's short grunts in the other room and by the time they'd returned the woman was already propped up in the bed again. "Child's dropped," the midwife said. "Hurry up now. Not long."

Mary handed over the towels and then, as directed, stood beside Mother Leeds wiping her head with a wet cloth. While the storm continued to fume and burst outside, the contractions increased and Leeds pushed along with the determined and positive instruction of the midwife. Thunder crashed again outside, exploding over the house.

The sheet that hung over the doorway moved some and Mary sensed several of the children hovering just outside, spying into the room. Over the rattling walls and gusting winds outside, she could make out more than one of them praying. They'd heard the same rumors in town.

"A bountiful head of hair," the midwife declared suddenly. "This is old happenings to you, Hannah. Musn't quit on me now." From where she stood, Mary couldn't see the baby's head yet, the face. Instead, she studied the midwife's face. Carefully searching for some clue, some indication, as to what the baby looked like. *She'd said it had bountiful hair, but did that same hair cover its entire face and body like some repulsive animal? Did it truly have horns and fangs, the face of the devil?*

The midwife's expression grew cross, anxious. It *is* the devil, Mary thought suddenly, pulling her hand away from Mother Leeds. "Let's get her on her side a bit, girls," the midwife directed calmly. Mary reached out again reluctantly and she and the two sisters shifted the woman slowly to her side. "Mary," the midwife called for her.

Mary's steps towards the end of the bed were heavy and slow. The girl kept her eyes to the floor as to not see the thing's face. "The shoulders 'ppear to be stuck," the midwife explained quietly. "On her side, we can turn the baby. Mary? Heed me now." Mary looked up. "Yes?"

"Yes." She shuddered and stole a look at the baby's face but now that the mother was turned, all she could see was the back of the head—wet and dark. The candlelight flickered, black shadows danced across the baby's form. Mary was unsure if she'd seen the demon's horns or not.

Moments later, it was born. "It's a boy," the midwife announced suddenly. *A boy? Not a demon,* Mary thought, shaking. The midwife had just claimed it to be so. There was a short cry, more like a yelp, from the thing and before Mary knew what had happened, it was all over.

She cut the cord at the midwife's direction, looking again for some sign that there was something wrong with the child, that the rumors had indeed been true. But in the dark room, she saw nothing but a small wet form passed to the Leeds woman.

The mother wept, clutching her new baby to her chest as the midwife gently rubbed its back. "Girls, take him now," she said. "Get him cleaned and swaddle him up nice and tight." The midwife looked up to the clattering roof. "It appears the storm's only getting started." She turned her attentions to the mother again, handing the baby over to Mary.

Mary held the newborn in her arms. It weighed almost nothing at all. She'd held babies before, of course, but none quite so small, quite so very new to this world. Nor quite so handsome, either. It was a fine looking baby for sure, she decided. Good color already with a nice round face and an adorable little nose. It hadn't quite opened its eyes yet, its mouth already

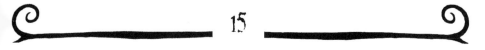

curling for milk.

Mary and the Leeds girls wiped the baby down slowly, wrapping him in a small blanket. The two sisters sniffled and sighed throughout. As the girls fussed over their new brother, Mary joined the midwife again for the remaining contractions and efforts of afterbirth. "Have one of the boys bury this, now," she ordered, and Mary marched back into the main room with the wooden bucket.

The second Leeds boy stood in her way when she came through the sheet. "Is it . . .?" His eyes dropped, looking for the right words.

"A baby boy," Mary told him. "He's just a . . . ." Now she too stopped mid-sentence, struggling to explain away the family's greatest suspicions and fears.

"Like us," the boy offered hopefully.

"Yes," she replied. "He's . . . just wonderful."

The boy turned to the other Leeds children who happily cast glances of genuine relief at each other. The oldest boy, the one who'd first questioned her at the door, watched her sorrowfully. Some aspect of the night, whether the fury of the storm, the delivery itself, or the obvious relief, had sobered whatever she'd seen in his eyes before. Only exhaustion covered his face now. He dropped his head into his hands and Mary suspected he was crying. She gave the bucket and instructions to the second boy, who stepped without argument, and with a bit of a spring, into the terrible storm waiting outside.

Mary smiled and turned back to the room where one of the smaller children, a young girl, stopped her. The girl held out something, and Mary took it. A baked yellow apple, sprinkled with cinnamon. "For my new brother," she explained. "I made it."

Mary giggled. "What a true and blessed sister you will be," she told her. "He's truly a lucky child." The Leeds girl beamed and skipped back to her spot before the fire.

Mary breathed deeply, half-convinced it was the first breath she'd taken since entering the house. Several of the sisters had carefully approached the eldest boy to comfort him and she returned to the backroom.

The baby lay still and quiet as Mother Leeds tried again for it to nurse. The midwife half looked on, finished cleaning up the room and giving instructions to the older sister. "Take one of the girls and help clean up in the other room." The midwife handed Mary a pile of sheets.

Then the second sister started screaming.

Mary turned and looked instinctively towards the bed.

The baby was *changing.*

In the space of moments, its nose and mouth had already drawn together, the upper lip merged into the tip of its nose. A single crude shape, an undistinguishable mound of bone and flesh now covered the child's face. As Mary watched in horror, the lump continued to grow. In the dim of candlelight, small bones cracked and skin ripped and the nose and jaws stretched

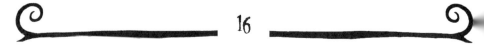

out further and further with each passing moment. The nostrils split, widened. The snout of some animal.

The ghastly mouth beneath the mound opened wide to scream, but no baby's cry would ever come from that horrible maw again. Instead the gnarled shrieks of the devil himself filled the backroom of the Leeds' home. High, piercing and jagged, like the screech of some horrific bird.

Its eyes opened wide, suddenly, and the baby looked directly at her. Strange, red eyes. Eyelids and cheeks peeled away. The face had become more angular and long, bones pulling and twisting the baby-pink skin in directions Mary hadn't thought possible.

The midwife yanked her backwards away from the bed and, for the first time, Mary was able to see the other changes. Its body had grown double in size already, a long dark serpent's tail springing from the blankets and spreading out now past the foot of the bed. What had once been small arms and hands were now long appendages ending in claws. The thing jabbed and scratched at its mother, her exposed skin tearing away as she screamed under the attack of her cursed thirteenth child. Hannah Leeds rolled away from the thing, but its body lay too close to hers and the hands reached out again, grabbing, pulling, digging at her. Deep cuts and scratches already covered her face, chest and arms.

"Kill it," one of the sisters shrieked. "Kill it!" She lunged at the creature, her hands curled into fists.

The thing leapt out at her, lifting from the bed. Its face latched onto her shoulder and there was a terrible crunch. Clawed fingers wrapped around her back, digging in deeper and more damaging wounds.

Mary stood rooted, frozen by the horror before her. She thought of something the midwife had said before they'd left for the Leeds home, something from the Bible. Many in the town already feared the child, suspected the worst, and openly hoped it would never be born. It had even been suggested that the midwife, herself, make sure the thing never took its second breath. To this, she'd snapped at her own husband: "And Pharaoh: declared 'If it be a son, you shall kill it but the midwives feared God and trusted in his unknown design and, so, would not do as Pharaoh commanded. And God blessed the midwives'." Before, Mary thought she'd understood the midwife's point, understood the role the two must play. But, what were they to do now?

It was then that the midwife fell upon the thrashing form, stuffing sheets over its face to smother the creature. It jerked and pressed beneath her as she held down even more tightly. "Help me, for God's sake!" she screamed. "Mary, help me!"

Mary stepped numbly forward, the world moving in slow motion around her as several of the other children rushed into the room. A range of screams and shouts joined the thunder rumbling outside, and where the shrieks began and the storm ended, she no longer recognized. She saw something that had once been feet. Hairy legs and hooves distending out of the blankets.

17

The creature expanded still, growing longer with each passing moment. It was now as long as the bed, as large as a full grown man. The thing rolled suddenly, flopping away from the bed to the floor behind it. Mary choked on her own scream. The long, glistening tail, like some giant snake, curled and slunk from under the bed. Strange animal snarls escaped from the shadowed darkness behind.

One of the boys rushed into the room, a short axe in his hands. Something dark lashed out at him, grabbing his neck, and the boy suddenly vanished, thrown back and below the bed. The axe landed on the floor with a loud thud.

The creature rose up, standing above the bed to its full height for the first time. In the darkened room, it looked to be Lucifer himself. The head was that of a horse. Angular and long, a huge snout. Its legs too had become the stump appendages of some herd animal, thick and hairy. It curled its arms just in front of a pink, hairless chest and middle. One hand still held onto the boy, *its brother*, the other seemed to reach across the room for Mother Leeds, who fell back and cringed against the furthest wall of the room.

Mary collapsed to her knees, shaking. Several indefinite forms moved in the darkness around her at various speeds and direction. The forms were the Leeds children, she now realized, trying to escape the massive snake tail as it lashed out across the room like some great whip, snapping out again and again. Each time, the lashes cut into one of the children and screams of agony now filled the house as bodies fell to the floor. The tail thrashed out again and the midwife also fell to the ground, tossed backwards like a cloth doll.

Several of the fallen children had stopped moving all together. The creature dropped the Leeds boy and fell upon one of the smaller bodies, one of its sisters, and began . . . began *feeding*. Wings, the wings of some monsterous bat, rose from its back.

"No!" Hannah Leeds wailed, spilling across the room towards the monster. Again the tail lashed out, striking her across the face, and her head whipped back, her nose broken and bloodied by the powerful whip. The woman pressed forward over the screams and shouting, over the storm that raged outside and the literal hell that now raged within her own home. Over the still bodies of her other children.

The creature stopped suddenly, its tail snaking out, coiling about behind it as it watched the Leeds woman. Its eyes, bulging round eyes that were neither animal nor human, shined red. It reached for the mother.

"No," she murmured. "My little boy, no." She fell against it, clinging to its waist and legs, pushing it away from the still body beneath them. The monster gazed about the room and watched the others scurrying for safety away from it. A strange cry, the most dreadful and mournful sound Mary had ever heard, rose from its horse-boned jaws.

"You're just my little boy," Mother Leeds sobbed. And Mary now knew that the woman did not speak of the child she'd just lost. But rather. . . .

The creature went still against her and Mother Leeds turned to the others. "My little boy,"

she said again to all of them. It was a declaration.

It was then that Mary realized she still held the apple. The treat the little Leeds girl has made so lovingly for her new baby brother, before it had become an actual demon from Hell. Whether that little girl was one of the children cowering behind her or one of the still dark forms on the floor, she did not know.

Mary sought the strength to stand and rose slowly, legs wobbling. The sound of the rain outside and the beast's heavy breaths filled the house as she ignored the sobs and groans of those around her.

If it be a son . . . "Mother Leeds?" she managed to croak out quietly. She stepped slowly, carefully, holding the apple out. Offering it to Mother Leeds or . . . . She wasn't sure. Mary only knew that in the world Leeds had just created, it was the one thing she could do.

The woman turned to study her. The creature, too, watched Mary with each step, the leathery wings flexing tautly behind its back. She dropped her eyes. "Mother Leeds," she said again and held the apple to her across the end of the bed. "Your daughter . . . ."

Something seized her hand and she gasped, falling away, but the thing held tight. She looked up, too terrified even to scream and saw that Hannah Leeds had grabbed her. The woman held her gaze, and Mary saw now that only madness remained in her eyes. A glossy-eyed distant madness that hinted at a world even darker and more horrifying than what she had just seen. Mary froze before it.

"Mary," it was the voice of the midwife that shook her awake again. "Come to me, now, Mary." She felt her hand released and turned away, moving back. The Leeds women fed the apple to Mary . . . .

The midwife wrapped her arm around Mary's shoulder, and she was tugged suddenly past the sheets through the doorway. Several of the children were already in the main room. Others followed just behind as the two outsiders staggered across the room and grabbed their cloaks. Strange sounds growled behind them again from the other room.

"Don't abandon us," one of the children, a small boy, cried out suddenly. His wide, terrified eyes had not yet left the curtain to the back room.

"Hurry, Mary," the midwife hissed as she tied Mary's cloak in place and made for the door.

"Nothing of this!" someone shouted. Mother Leeds, herself, had staggered after them and now hovered just past the doorway of the bedroom. Her children, those who still lived, stood silent before the fire, trembling. "You say nothin' of this," she warned flatly. "Nothin'."

The midwife turned to her wide-eyed. She collected Mary to her side again and stumbled backwards towards the front door.

"A child born with . . . with such 'deformity'," Mother Leeds managed, "That's a suspicious matter."

Mary felt her neck squeezed tightly, being dragged across the room.

"And midwives of such children have been oft accused of witchcraft." Leeds finished her thought.

"I understand," the midwife said without turning and pushed open the door to the waiting storm outside.

Mary stole a final look into the house. Most of the children had turned their attentions back to the fire, lost already to the ghastly memories of the night and the sinister future their mother had just set before them. Mother Leeds retreated without another word back to the bedroom. Back to those who had already died. And, back to her new baby.

The midwife yanked Mary into the storm, the rain and wind assaulting her face and the two women stumbled away from the house into the darkness. Tall black pines loomed above her, waving in the harsh winds. She ran as fast as her legs would let her and tried with all her might to keep up as the dark forest swallowed them both.

When they were half a mile away, they stopped, and the midwife fell to her knees. Neither the roar of the snarling winds or the rolling grumble of thunder could completely hide her screams.

Overgrown with milkwort and cottongrass, most wouldn't even recognize it as a trail. But, Mary Hillman knew the way well and moved surely, though slowly, towards the house once again. She stopped when she reached the broken front gate which marked the border of the main yard. The grounds were wild and seedy and had been for many years now. The house itself long abandoned, a back corner of its shingled roof caved in. She watched it for a long time, catching her breath and feeling the warm sun on her face. She closed her eyes briefly, allowed certain memories to return. From sixty-two years before.

Mary reached into the basket, pulled out the apple, baked just that morning, and sprinkled with cinnamon. She placed it, as she did each year, next to the post and surveyed the grounds again. Took in the blackened windows, the dark corners through water-rotted walls and broken shutters. Watched the endless secretive pines that surrounded the home like an army of shadows from some darker time.

"Happy birthday," she said, softly.

A sudden chill in the air forewarned a fall storm brewing off the coast that could suddenly find its way across the Barrens. Mary started the long walk home.

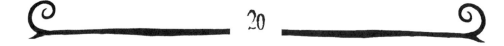

NOTES: The birth itself is probably the most-recounted Jersey Devil story, and 1735 is considered the actual birth year in almost every version. In some accounts, the midwives themselves are among the creature's first victims. Several names have been attributed to its mother, but the name most commonly used, by far, is "Mother Leeds."

It was once believed that evil spirits were attracted to people on their birth day, and to protect them from harm, friends and family would visit the birth day person with good thoughts, wishes, and gifts. That same custom became today's birthday celebrations.

LIVING IN DARKNESS
1738

what? what run . . . man!
manboy. manboy run. many boy run.
chase manboy. hide? no . . . food. many food.
many. yell. manboy fast. many hit . . . hit manboy.
hit. hate many. manboy out. run. run.
brother.

Daniel Leeds ran for his life. He ignored the burning in his chest and the throbbing lump that now filled the right side of his face. He ignored the split lip and dripping nose, the distinct taste of blood in his mouth. He thought only of keeping his legs moving one more step, one more step.

The sandy soil, soft under his frantic sprint, kicked out from his leather boots, the other boys falling back some. Their shouted curses and threats still hung just behind his heels though. He no longer heard the exact words as they'd become only garbled growls lost behind his own rapid breath. But, he knew their meaning well enough.

He glanced to the side through long blond bangs, looking for the others. They'd encircled him once already, and he swore that would never happen again. The sunlight spread long narrow shadows in every direction, the sun hot on his back. He darted between two white cedars, breaking hard to the left away from the small mob pursuing him. There were three of the Watson brothers; Heath, Benjamin and Jed; and also Nathan Cramer and Todd Mulliner. The group had caught him out fishing, and he'd almost gotten away again. But there were two more boys this time, the Cox brothers, and he'd been chased right into a trap.

Before, Jonathon might have helped him. But his older brother had long since gone. They were all gone now, William and Joseph, too. And his own father's face was no longer even a faint memory. Jonathon had joined up with one of the fishing boats just six months before, and Daniel figured to never see him again. His brother wanted him to come too, but Daniel couldn't leave his mother and sisters. In just four years, he'd gone from the third youngest child to, at the age of nine, the eldest man of the house.

Daniel caught sight of his property. Another hundred steps and he'd be through the trees at last and up the short path to the house. The shouts behind him grew more agitated, eager. No one came too close to the house anymore.

Daniel sensed an anxious burst of speed from his pursuers, perhaps a last effort before they'd turn back, and risked a look behind. Benjamin Watson was just behind now, his face red and angry, one hand stretched out to grab him.

The screech filled the woods then. A shrill cry that grew progressively higher until it had reached a truly ghastly pitch. It hovered on that macabre tone for several seconds, the note warbling like some demonic bird for far too long, coming out finally in piercing, choked sounds that carried the shriek all the way back down into the low-throated rumble and purr of a cougar or wolf.

Daniel ignored the cry as best he could. He'd heard it so many times before. The others had as well, but only from afar, deep in the woods and late at night; laying awake in their beds, the covers pulled close, as their mothers added wood to the fire and their fathers checked the musket powder. They stumbled to a complete stop.

"We'll get you, runt!" Heath Watson screamed after him, the other boys already retreating back into the woods. "You and that demon of yours!"

Daniel ran past another thicket of trees, the evil house looming closer still.

"I ain't scared, you hear me!" Heath shouted back into the woods, steadily backing away.

"We'll come back with more men!" He turned, chasing after his gang. "And then we'll get all of you!" he rang out, his voice vanishing again into the pines.

Daniel kept running, hopping through their half-empty vegetable garden towards the front door. Just to his right, the creature perched atop the fence.

The demon crouched so that its shaggy chest lay flat against the knees, its full weight balanced over one of the posts. The massive wings lay close to its back, pressed against the gruesome shape, and a long tail coiled down and around the post, ending in a slowly flickering, pointed tip. Its long angular face, the face of a horse, hung over its knees, and its glistening eyes watched Daniel pass.

The boy was not surprised to see the monster there. It often watched them from that post.

It returned every few weeks, in fact, to stalk the house and the dwindling family within. It crouched mostly silently, and motionless, watching them, as Daniel and the others hid in the house, huddled together in shadowed corners or under beds.

Fear and dread now blanketed his very spirit and most of him just wanted to collapse on the ground before the beast, to curl tightly into a horrified ball. Instead, Daniel ran through the chill that gripped him wholly and made it to the door. The boy found it locked tight as he'd expected. He rapped frantically at the door. "It's me," he whispered. "Open up."

"Daniel?" A small voice from the other side of the door.

"Yes, Deborah, quickly now." He heard the latches lifted and pushed the door open,

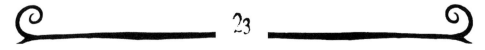

jumping into the house. He braced the door again and turned into the living room. "Where are the others?"

"Upstairs," his sister told him. Her eyes were dark and drained, and he could tell she'd been crying again. "We heard someone screaming." Her eyes roamed over his battered face. "We kept waiting for you to get back."

"Well, and so here I am," he held out his arms and tried to smile.

"Oh, Daniel," she touched his cheek and he winced. "They been after you again. The Watsons."

"Maybe, but you should see how bad *they* look." He chuckled and the sudden movement pained his bruised ribs.

Deborah shook her head. "What happened now?" she asked quietly, afraid of his answer.

"Some fool over in Tuckerton," he said. "Gone missing. They found some blood, though."

"Lord, help us." Her eyes turned unconsciously to the fireplace. "What have we done?"

Daniel followed her gaze to the gaping black hole, now filled with the blaze of a midday fire, and shuddered. The monster had escaped the house through that same hole almost three years before. That's when the disappearances and killings had started.

That very night, babies vanished from their cribs and chicken coops were ripped to pieces. Weeks later, an entire family had disappeared from their cabin, leaving no trace, and over the next few seasons, several children from Brotherton to Mays Landing were said to have vanished. Two had been found, but their remains, like those of the mutilated mules and goats that'd been found, were no longer recognizable. Right away, there'd been little debate as to the monster's name or identity.

Many had already heard of the "Leeds Devil," the deformed child that Mother Leeds kept locked in her cellar. It was said to be the very spawn of the Devil, and that it had killed the father and several of the Leeds children. Daniel would not deny these things.

In the cellar, it had dwelled for almost a year. The night it was born, Mother had led it down the steps somehow and locked the thing into the darkness below. While Daniel and the others hid behind the older children, Mother Leeds stayed down in the basement with it for some time. But when she came back up, she'd barred the basement door and had Joseph put another door over the first.

Daniel always suspected it could have broken out the cellar door anytime it wanted to, but something kept it inside, some promise of his mother perhaps. It lived off the rain water that seeped into the cellar and whatever bugs or rodents had burrowed inside. Daniel knew his mother crept down some nights too, brought the demon food and whispered to it. It lived there in total darkness and just above, the children could hear its screeching, as it moved about the room each day, scratching at the walls, growling in high-pitched snarls and thrashing about the cellar.

Until the night it got out.

It had pushed past mother and Joseph, breaking off the second cellar door and stepping into the kitchen. Screams had filled the house, and Daniel remembered being pushed towards the front door.

"Protect the door," Mother had shouted at them all. "For God's sake, we can't let him out." Daniel remembered stumbling towards the door, unsure of what, if anything, he might do to stop the massive beast. Everything became quick uneven movements and shadow. Even now, Daniel couldn't remember much of what had happened that night. He remembered that more screams had filled the cottage. And that Joseph had spilled into the room, unmoving.

Daniel had never seen the beast until then. It had been kept in the cellar for so long, since the night it was born. It blinked, stepping into the room, its bulging, animal eyes fluttering in the lantern-lit cottage. A year in complete darkness, Daniel thought. Its every day and night becoming one long night in that dark cellar.

Its body was gaunt and covered in coarse hair, and it had the skeletal ribs and chest of a grown man, wiry dark legs. It lumbered further into the room, the legs wide, its monstrous eyes in the huge horse head glaring at the children trapped inside.

"Baby," Mother cried. "Come to mother, baby!" She stepped towards it with her arms held out as if to hug the creature. It roared at her, leaning forward, its great muzzle sputtering foam and spit across the room, opening wide enough for Daniel to see the sharp teeth within its cavernous jaws.

Then, the demonic, equine head turned suddenly to Daniel and the door. The hunched shaggy shoulders rolling awkwardly. In the chaos, other children stepped between them, and he couldn't truly see the beast straight on. By the time they'd moved again, the creature had turned towards the empty chimney and scampered up into it.

It jumped headfirst right into the opening, the wings laid flat against its shaggy back, hind legs kicking up into the darkness. The harsh sounds of its struggles up the chimney echoed down into the room and the children had huddled together, shaking in fear. Daniel, however, had remained against the front door as he'd been told, only now watching his mother's face as the pointed tail at last slipped into the chimney's darkness.

He'd heard it again outside, thrashing down the side of the house and, at last, its sounds echoed into the night. It cried out then, the shrillest and loudest call it had ever yet made, amplified all the more now that it was outside. The shriek rolled across the Barrens and rose up finally to the very moon itself.

Now, Daniel looked away from the fire place, pushing back the illusion, the memory, of a dark pointed tail hanging out of the opening, coiling over the mantel. No, he assured himself. That's what the fire is for. We must never let the fire out again. "How long has it been there?" he asked his sister Deborah.

"Since just after you left," she said. "It hasn't moved." She trembled when she spoke. Her

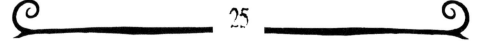

eyes, to Daniel, looked like the eyes of some the old men who worked down on the fishing boats, and he had to remind himself she was only ten herself.

"Check on the others," he told her. "I need to talk with mother."

She nodded silently and padded off through the kitchen towards the second floor. He watched her go and shuddered as she passed the cellar door. He hated that door, hated the whole cellar. He'd looked down into it only once before, years ago when William had passed on, and had sworn to never look again. The absolute darkness of the room was alive somehow; malevolent even, and filled with such pain and evil that he dared not look into its horrid blackness again. It was as if the demon had never escaped at all.

Daniel turned away and crossed the floor to toss another log onto the fire. He briefly warmed his trembling hands over the colorful flames, though his fingers remained icy and numb. There was blood on his one hand, and he wiped it off on his pants.

He moved across the room to stand in the bedroom's doorway. His heart started pounding again. They didn't go into that room much anymore either.

His mother sat in the far corner, half-cast in shadow, hunched beside the window. She swayed back and forth slowly in the chair. Her arms were crossed tightly, hugging herself, as she rocked before him, staring out into the yard. Her whispered mumbles sounded to Daniel only as autumn leaves falling through the higher branches, hollow and seemingly endless.

He glanced at the strange images on the walls. Pictures and letters his mother had scrawled over the last few years. Hexes of protection, he told himself, but the strange letters and symbols gave such a horrid feeling, he knew he was only fooling himself. The drawings were so awful he couldn't even look at them.

Closer now, he could see the scratches on her arms and face. Long scabs, spotted and dark, criss-crossed her pale skin. Faded scars of earlier cuts ran beside them.

"Mother?" he said softly.

Her mouth hung half open in her mutterings, her eyelids heavy and unmoving.

"There's been another killing," he said. "Another child."

She stared ahead, perhaps trying to ignore his words.

"Mother."

"They blame him for everything now," she said quietly, staring past the window. "If some goat . . . some child gets killed, someone's crops go bad, they . . . they blame *him*." Her words were garbled and low, and Daniel watched her, trembling. "Shipwrecks, miscarriages, hailstorms . . . ."

"We need to move away," he said. "Just leave this place, this bad place, forever."

"They know who to blame now, don't they? The 'Leeds Devil.'"

"Lilith's down in Willington, she and her husband."

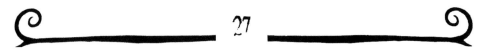

"Lilith?" she repeated the name slowly.

The boy clenched his fists. "Lilith, Mother. Lilith." His eldest sister had moved away soon after the birth, and they hadn't seen her since. He wasn't even sure if she was in Willington, but it was as good a start as any. A start away from Leeds Point.

"Can't leave," his mother said. "Too late for that."

"Then you have to make it leave, mother. Just make it go away!"

She turned to him slowly, the empty eyes falling upon him fully. "I can't," she said. He's coming back home is all. How . . . how can I stop such a thing as that?"

"You feed him, Mother," he said. "I know you do. I seen you sneak out at night."

She moaned almost. "I . . . He must eat. If I don't, he'll . . . ."

Find something else to eat, he finished the thought, but offered another. "That's when he scratches you," he said aloud. "Isn't it?"

She slowly brought her hand to her face and drew it along one of the deep scars there. "He doesn't know what he's doing," she said more to herself. "Still so young. So, I try . . . pray for him to be . . . to be a good boy again."

Daniel wiped the hair from his eyes. "I'll kill it for hurting you," he snarled.

She smiled weakly. "You're not . . . you can't kill him. Not him."

Daniel knew she was right. At least not alone, I can't, he thought. His mother mumbled something incomprehensible. "Mother?"

"Tell . . . tell Henry to finish clearing out the hollow."

"Henry's gone mother. He kilt himself two years ago, now. Jonathon, William, and Constance are gone too. Joseph . . . ." He paused, thinking of the night it'd escaped, the night Joseph passed on too. He then shook off the memory of the others who'd been killed the night it was born. "Ain't no one left but me, Deborah, Eileen, and Grace. Ain't no one left."

Her vacant expression stared ahead.

"Sometimes," he said, toeing the dusty floor. "Sometimes at night, I lay awake and I think. I think that, I wish that, sometimes, that I was like him." He leaned towards the window and looked out at the dark shape on the post. "I wish that it'd whisper a spell to me or something like that and then I'd change. I'd have wings too, and those fangs. I'd be a monster just like him and then . . . ."

His mother's breathing had slowed beside him and the room had grown terrifyingly quiet.

"Then I wouldn't be afraid no more. Not of the Watsons or about what was gonna happen to us, or about him. I wouldn't be afraid of anything."

"He's scared," she whispered. "A mother knows. Oh, so very scared."

"Maybe," Daniel said. "But, we'd have each other then. And with the two of us, neither

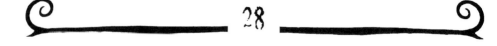

one of us need be scared again. And if I was like that, if I was more like him." He studied her glazed expression, her eyes only for the demon hovering on the post just outside their house. "Maybe you'd . . ." he said, his voice choking some. "Maybe, then."

He reached a hand out, the back of his fingers moving against her arm. Mother Leeds remained staring straight ahead, and a cloud must have crossed the sun then, because her face was suddenly covered completely in shadow. "So very scared," she said again.

Daniel took his hand away and cleared his throat. "I've got to go out again, Mother," he said. "There's some chores I have to take care of."

"Remember," she said again. "Tell Henry to finish the hollow."

"Yes, Mother," Daniel replied softly. "I will."

The Leeds boy led a small army back through the pines. There were the three Watson brothers again, and also Nathan Cramer and Todd Mulliner. The Cox brothers had recruited an older uncle too. Between them, they had four good rifles and two axes.

They'd beaten Daniel pretty badly when he'd come to them and had almost drowned him before he'd gotten the words out in a way that made sense to them. I'll help you, he'd shouted, tears burning in his eyes. I'll help you kill the demon once and for all.

"We don't need your help," Heath Watson had spit, kicking him again. Cruel, for sure, but not stupid, he'd listened finally to Daniel's whole plan. Now, they crouched back in the woods, just beyond the boundary of the house. Their eyes were wide, hands shaking. Just through those trees, the devil himself waited for them.

Someone's shout suddenly lifted through the trees. It was an angry voice just ahead of them. "What's that," Nathan Cramer choked.

"I'll go," Daniel whispered. "But," he held up a musket pistol, one his father had left behind. "You've got to come out as soon as I shoot."

The others looked at each other.

"Got to surround him," Daniel continued, looking back at his house strangely. "We can't let it out."

There were few nods, and Daniel expected half of them would bolt right then and there. He turned from them and moved through the last wall of trees into the yard.

The creature remained atop the post. Standing taller than usual, hissing at something in front of it. Daniel passed another tree, then stopped.

His mother stood directly before the monster, waving her arms and shouting. The demon merely watched her, bobbing up and down slowly on the post.

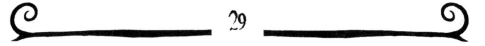

"Go!" she shouted at it, "Never come back!" She threw something at it, a rock, and it slammed into the dark shape's side before bouncing again to the ground.

His mother crouched down again and picked up another rock. "Go away, I said!" she yelled again, her voice cracking as she stood up straight. "I don't want you!" Another rock flew from her hand, hitting the thing in the snout. The creature shrieked at her in warning, a piercing cackle that sputtered to a high-pitched growl.

"You're bad. Go away!" she shrilled. Her voice was racked in sobs. She looked suddenly around the yard and then marched across it to pick something up. She charged the fence again with an old hand plow. She swung the plow at the creature and the pole thudded against its hairy shape with a sickening crunch. "Leave us be!" she shouted and pulled back the plow to strike again.

The demon leapt from the post suddenly and dropped directly in front of Mother Leeds. It rose to its full height in front of her, then lowered its massive head to hover right above her. Daniel screamed, unsure if any sound had actually come out, and started moving towards the nightmare before him.

The creature's jaws opened, slowly lifting back to reveal its rows of jagged teeth. The horse snout pulled wider apart until the mouth was big enough to wrap completely about his mother's head. The fangs now framed the top of her head and her chin, its saliva dripping in the gaping black between. A purring growl rose from its dark throat.

His mother had closed her eyes, standing still before the monster. She held the plow limply at her side now. "Please," she managed. "You must go."

Daniel stumbled finally into the yard, and the thing turned to face him directly. As it had four years before, but now there was no one between them.

He lifted the gun.

The creature lunged at him, and Daniel squeezed his hand tight. The pistol fired in a plume of smoke. In two massive hops, the demon crossed the yard and appeared in the smoke's cloud, just in front of him. It shrieked again, and Daniel fell to the ground, eyes closed, covering his ears vainly against the piercing sound.

The boy felt his body being lifted, sharp nails digging into his back, pulling him from the ground. The gun dropped from his hand, and the thing turned him around, clutching Daniel in its talons. Daniel's back burned as the claws scratched deeper into his skin. He kept his eyes closed, scrunched tight against the nightmare.

Its breath blew hot and rank against his face, gummy spit dripping down his neck and chest. Daniel tried breathing from his mouth, but it only came out as a choked scream. The demon's panting and rumblings were closer still, filling the boy's entire reality. It breathed steadily, holding him close, the claws digging more painfully into his skin.

Then, the monster snorted, and hot air literally seared Daniel's face. In pain, he opened his eyes again, screaming in the face of the dark monster holding him.

A single eye held him fast.

The demon's eye was round, both dark and evil, a fat obsidian jewel from a time before men, a place without light. The cellar, Daniel thought distantly. It's just like looking down into the cellar. Then the eyes grew darker still, and even more evil.

It dropped him, and Daniel's body slumped to the ground. The thing screeched again, and its wings opened wide. It hopped clumsily above, hovering like a ghostly black crane, and its garbled breathing filled the yard in ragged gasps. Then, it flapped the wings once more and vanished into the forest.

Deborah burst from the house, flying across the yard, and crashed at his side. The other Leeds children hovered in the shadowed doorway. "Daniel," she cried. "Daniel!"

"I had to," her mother sobbed just behind them. "I had to. They was going to kill him. Kill my baby boy."

Deborah turned back to the still shape beside her.

His body was unnaturally slack, mouth hanging half-open. "Daniel," his sister prodded, tapping at his chest. "Daniel?" She pulled him closer.

His gaze remained completely vacant, the black pupils now filling his eyes.

"It's gone, Daniel," Deborah whispered to him. Tears filled her eyes now. "It's truly gone. Everything's going to be fine. I . . . Daniel?"

Daniel Leeds only murmured softly.

girl. sister? happy girl? cry girl

trees. sun . . .

many boy run. woods. many yelling.

boys fast. run in woods. run . . . he flies

sound. his voice. he caught boys.

brother.

NOTES: The Leeds family was one of the most popular and powerful of pre-colonial New Jersey. A Leeds, for instance, was the first Surveyor General of West Jersey and another the first mayor of Atlantic City. Their political and business notoriety may certainly have contributed to the name ultimately selected for the legendary monster (It was popular to vilify the rich and powerful in 1735, too). There are hundreds of Leeds descendants living in New Jersey still today and thousands across the United States.

LEGION

1740

Father Garner caught his breath and laid a hand against the crucifix and silver vial hung over his chest. Inside the ornate cylinder was a relic, a bone shard of Saint Martin de Tours, the Glory of Gaul. For tonight, a needed saint of soldiers.

The Jesuit's guide, a middle-aged Huron named Mononcue, stood beside him holding their lantern. The Indian wore the traditional deerskin shirt, breechcloths, fringed leggings, and moccasin shoes of his tribe. A broad bow and full quiver of arrows ran across his back. He'd walked with Father Garner for more than a year, sharing his burden. But tonight he'd run, chasing after this newest, darkest spirit.

The devil now waited for them at the top of the hill. It stood against a cloud-greyed dawn, the tall trees' night shadows still creeping across the hillside.

"He is done running," the priest said in his native French. He'd crossed the sea ten years before to minister to the Indian tribes in Canada, and had slowly moved down the Eastern coast of the new world with the Huron people and among the English settlers, enemies of his church and his native land. He was young, in his early thirties, and had deep blue eyes and long black hair that curled from under the wide brim of his *cappello romano*. He looked up the hill with his guide as the creature weaved between two trees, stooping in the dreary morning's shadows. Strange lights, like faint azure flashes of lighting, shimmered behind it.

"It is a black thing," Mononcue said, also in French. "A *deghseerenoh*. We should not go forward."

Garner studied his guide, a man who'd proven himself as brave as any man the priest had ever met. And, yet, Mononcue had purposely used the Huron word for evil spirit, warning of darkness older than the devil himself. And, he'd earlier cautioned Garner that local tribes, those of the Leni Lenape, called the area *Squanqum*, the "place of the evil god." If *this* man is afraid . . . .

The priest glanced back up the hill and saw the barbed wings and snout again, the demon's tail. Evil god. "I must," he said simply.

The Huron nodded. "Then, I must."

Garner smiled and squeezed the Monocue's arm, then turned again to the demon above them. *"Tu autem effugare, diabole. Appropinquabit enim judicium Dei,"* He whispered in Latin, *Be gone, Devil. The judgment of God is at hand.* He unclasped his black calf-length cape, revealing the short sword at his hip.

The Huron took the cape and laid it carefully upon the ground while Garner searched through his own bag. The priest withdrew a silver bell and several vials and stuffed them in his sash, then took out a candle and the Book of the Law. He opened the tome and laid a slip of paper into it, setting the book onto his laid-out cape. He then lit the candle from the lantern. *"Exorcizo te, omnis spiritus immunde, in nominee Dei."* He crossed himself with the candle, another exorcism begun.

Vials were opened and the sword was anointed with oil, *"Ego to linio oleo salutis in_ Christo Domino nostro,"* and holy water. He quietly recited the Paternoster and the 54th psalm, then started up the hill with the sword.

The thing moved, weaving quickly through the trees towards him, scurrying on two hind legs. It was dark, covered in coarse black hair, and its tail and wings whipped behind it like one of hell's bat-eared dragons as it raced down the short hill. The crooked arms bobbled before its chest, stunted in length, ending in massive clawed hands.

Garner slowed in his steps. Though he'd been chasing the fiend all night, it was the first time he'd truly seen it. In the cold uncompromising dawn, he saw that this was not some minor demon, or a possessed and disfigured human. It was the very Devil himself.

Father Rye had once described a demon he'd encountered named Buer, a beast shaped like a pentagram, five hoofed legs growing from its horrible lion-like face. The old Jesuit had recounted his fear to Garner, expressing a terror born of this thing that was not of this world, but something from the ninth circle that had driven the priest almost to madness. Almost, Father Rye had winked. And then he'd told Garner what had gotten him through the horror.

Garner breathed deeply, and brought the sword up again with both hands. *"Credo,"* he hissed, closing his eyes and remembering the old Jesuit's counsel. "I believe."

He opened his eyes again and slashed the blessed sword towards the fiend. "I am upon thee," he recited in Latin. "Thou shalt not stand before me!"

The demon reared back, skidding on the dewed pine needles and leaves, and then stood still, watching him. Its neck turned, the grotesque head cocked curiously, and the black eyes bored into his own.

Father Garner's legs trembled, but his voice was clear and grew stronger with each word. "Thou hast rejected the Truth and I spew thee out! I cast thee into the Abyss! I command thee to withdraw and depart, without further delay!"

The devil's snout turned up some, a lean smile of sharp fangs. The stench from the thing was sulfuric and foul, and Garner gagged on the start of his next line. "Return now from whence you came, and come not again unless summoned. Be gone, I say, in the name of God!" With the sword, he quickly made the sign of the cross.

It sprang at him.

The Jesuit brought the ceremonial blade up in defense just as the creature fell upon him. Its hands stretched out for his face, black talons curled and splinted. The blade blocked the thing's attack, and Garner fell against the terrible weight and force of the beast, crashing backwards to the ground.

Garner's head thumped off the forest floor, and his arms flung to the sides, the sword dropping several paces away. The thing now hovered directly above him, staring at its hand, its wounded hand, the hairy legs straddling each side of the prone priest. Garner felt the thing's bulk and heat against his legs. "*Tu autem . . .*" he sputtered. "*Tu autem effugare, diabole.*"

The beast leaned closer, the mutilated and distended head and face looming, now, just above his own. Its breath was hot and growling, rancid with stink. He saw another flash of its fangs and a long forked tongue darting over the edge of its dark black lips.

"*App. . . appropinquabit enim judicium Dei, enim judicium Dei . . .*"

It leaned deeper until the dreadful black eyes were just above Garner's own. Its eyes flashed red suddenly, a sparkle of flame and malice passing through them. "*Credo,*" the Frenchman whispered. "*Credo.*"

The jaws opened with a deep snarl, rank saliva dripping into the priest's face, rows of sharp fangs filling Garner's whole world.

A horrible sound filled his mind then, the thing's wet breath spewing in his face. It was a shriek so ghastly, he started screaming himself as the black form lifted away, the shape and weight pulling off his trembling body. Another shape appeared beside him, dancing and shouting. He heard the demon scrambling away, crashing through underbrush away from them. "Amen," Garner gasped and rolled for the sword.

"It's gone," a voice said in French.

Garner grabbed his sword and looked up at Mononcue. The Huron walked over, his eyes ever on the demon above them, and held out a bronzed arm to help Garner back up. "Merci," the priest said. "I . . ." He laughed. "*Merci*, Mononcue."

"*Oneghekewishenoo,*" The Huron grinned, holding up his bow. "I have conquered my enemy."

"Your blessed bow," Father Garner repeated the words the Huron had said to him often, his heart finally slowing in his chest.

Mononcue nodded. "The *haotong* told me it would prove very powerful." They stared up the hill and watched as the demon's shape jerked and swayed among the shadowed trees. Several sharp cries barked out again over the hilltop and Garner shuddered, remembering the demon's original cry of pain. The thing vanished over the hillside.

"We shall follow it?" Mononcue asked.

"No," Garner shook his head. "We should not. Our blessed weapons are not . . . Praise God we could defend ourselves. But, I fear . . ." Garner dropped his eyes to the ground.

Mononcue tapped his arm. "Father Garner?"

 34

The Jesuit turned and watched a hunched dark shape moving towards them from the west. The crooked form was black and shaggy, and seemed to float through the pines, coming nearer.

"Now what deviltry?" Garner's grip redoubled on his sword. The figure glided closer still, and he saw now that the figure was human, cloaked in animal skin.

"*Utchke*," Mononcue murmured. "A woman. Leni Lenape."

Garner now saw that the cloak was a black wolf-skin coat that went over the head, a colorful woven-sash around her neck held a wide pouch and flowers adorned her robe and leggings. She carried only a turtle-shell rattle and jiggled it softly. "She is *meteinuwak*," the Huron guide explained. "A medicine woman. Magical."

They met her at the bottom of the hill, standing around Garner's cloak, the service candle still burning. Up close, her face was young and bright, and Garner figured she was no older than twenty. She smiled at them both, her dark eyes cheerful, and bowed slightly. The two men bowed back, and the three attempted introductions in various languages. English proved the easiest to manage. "What are you doing here?" Garner began.

The girl, called Esaw, covered a narrow smile with her painted hand. "Same as you, holy man. My people call this *Shamong*, the horned place, or *Sqaunqum*, the . . . ."

"The place of the evil god," he finished.

"Yes," she nodded slowly. "I feel your battle."

"Feel?" Father Garner looked at Mononcue, then turned back to the girl. "You are a *meteinuwak*."

She nodded. "Through prayer and visions, I speak these energies. All things in world have life spirits, the *menetuwak*. These made by *Kishelemukong*, the Creator. I feel the battle at start of night and have followed you. Help you."

Father Garner's eyes narrowed. "Help?"

She nodded and held up the ornate rattle. "I have, how say, guarded the hill. Net of light around other side. It can not leave."

"It's trapped." Garner blinked. "Net of light? You mean, you used magic?"

She looked deliberately at his candle and book, and then at the vial and cross around his neck. "That English word for it?" she replied, smiling softly and his eyes narrowed. "You kill creature?" she asked.

"No," he shook his head. "To exorcise it, to save its soul. We were to take a boat from Leeds Point down into Maryland when I heard the tale of the child, the deformed and lost child. The people would not go near it."

"The *Yuhavitam*," she smiled. "The People of the Pines. They are afraid of it. They know its evil. There are many dark spirits inside this bad thing," she said, and for the first time her eyes grew dark and worried. "These are evil woods, old woods, filled with much dark spirits. Much spirits in this *menetuwak*."

"Yes," Garner nodded at her, pleased, and looked up the hill. "The son of my god once battled a possessed man, and when he asked the foul spirit its name," he paused and scratched his beard thoughtfully. "The demon replied, 'Legion, for we are many.' This is what I exorcise tonight."

"*Exorcise?*"

"To force the demon within to swear an oath, to behave. Can this be done, Esaw?" Garner asked, glancing at her. "Can it be forced to behave?"

"Or can it be killed?" Mononcue's soft question floated between him. Garner nodded. Yes. If necessary. He would do that.

The Leni Lenapi sighed, her mouth in a frown. "I think no," she said softly. "Many *Meteinuwak* have tried before. *Meteinuwak* died. Your sword?"

"No," Garner shook his head. "The Blade of Revealing is to only hold it for awhile," he said. "And even then . . . ." He thought again of the fiend crashing against him.

"It will break," she replied. "Like our magic guards of light. Always."

"It is written in Matthew that I have been given the power against unclean spirits, and yet, I could not stop it."

"Your 'magic' is very strong," she said.

He sighed. "It is your faith that holds it now."

"Only for little time," she said. "Faith of one woman maybe not enough."

He studied her face, detailed paint across her cheeks and forehead, festooned bone and nuts strung through her hair beneath the wolf-skin head. "Or, of one man," he said. He thought of the magical lights holding the demon at bay.

"Yes," she smiled. "That is why I find you. We hold it and command to stop the evil. We have its 'oath'?"

"For a thousand years," Garner determined, tapping the relic around his neck. "An oath of peace that will last a thousand years." He studied the Indian woman again, then slowly lifted his sword and held it straight before him. "*Qui*," he said. Esaw laid her own turtle-shell rattle across the blade, and the two looked at the Huron, who lowered his bow so that the three blessed items crossed each other. "Maybe," Garner said.

"*Qui*," Esaw replied. "Maybe."

Mononcue's eyes widened. "It turns night again," he said. "See?"

Father Garner had not. But, now, as he looked up the hill and into the sky, he understood his companion's warning. The sky had indeed grown darker, night seeming to fall upon the forest again as the sun vanished behind baleful clouds.

"They will come soon," Esaw whispered.

"Who?" He asked, "Who will come?"

She turned and her gaze had become distant and somber. "The, how to say, shadow people," she replied. "Men of shadow."

Garner and Mononcue looked at each other, eyes narrow and confused. Before the Jesuit could ask anything further, the devil shrieked from the top of the hill. The three allies moved closer together, joining against the hellish sound, and Father Garner steadied himself with their company. The Leeds Devil charged again.

Its loping run quickly became more of cramped, frenzied scuttle. Hunched over again on four legs, it tore down the hill even faster then before. The speed alone chilled Garner's mind, froze him with dread. The gristled wings flapped slowly above it, helping its charge.

"It try to pass," Esaw breathed. "We stop it."

Mononcue let loose the first arrow and the bolt struck the monster clear in the chest. But the bolt and feathers passed cleanly through the thing's back and wings as if it had passed through only the wind, and the arrow flew another twenty paces before skittering to the ground. The Huron had already notched and fired another. It too passed through the devil.

By now it was virtually on them. The Indian lunged forward and stabbed his bow's pointed tip into the pouncing brute. The two shapes slammed together in a ferocious flare of sound. There was a horrible cry again as the tip of the bow sunk deep into the beast.

The thing turned violently against the Huron's stab, and Mononcue stumbled sideways away from the creature. The demon pulled its hairy hands to the wound, head turned in agony, and the long black tail stretched over its head to coil around the Indian's neck. Mononcue's bow skittered to the forest floor, and he was lifted towards the thing's gaping jaws. Then, the beast stopped.

Garner now heard the rattle beside him, Esaw's turtle-shell rattle. At first, it was a low clatter, only recognizable because it seemed the one sound in the forest that wasn't violent and ghoulish. Gradually, the sound increased, and he heard its exotic rhythm, found a cadence that grew louder and more defined with each moment.

Mononcue had been dropped to the ground, and Garner watched the Leeds Devil back slowly from the medicine woman's rattling, from her magic.

Its wings fanned out behind it, spreading wide so that its blackness filled the space of several men. The head reared back, the sickening snout opening atop the contorted neck, and then snapped forward again. Fire sprang from its mouth, spurting a budding streak of uneven flames towards her. The blaze screamed and hissed like a thousand lost voices.

"*In nominee Dei*," the words rushed from Garner's mouth over the horrible hiss, and his sword thrust between the demon's fiery breath and the Indian girl. "*Exorcizo te, omnis spiritus immunde*," he swung the sword against the flames, and the fire literally curved away from his blade. Heat rolled painfully across his face, but the flames did not touch him. Esaw fell back against him.

"*Et in noi mine Jesu Christi!*" the priest roared, and the blade swung downward into the retreating fire. The demon stepped back, its black gullet widening as a finer line of flame poured out.

"*In virtute Spiritus Sancti,*" he swung the blade a final time left to right, completing the sign of the cross as the flames burst against the sword. There was a sudden flash of light, and hot embers exploded in every direction.

The Leeds Devil hopped backwards, its wings lifting it in reverse several feet. It shrieked, a high-pitched garble that sounded far too human for Garner's ears or faith to accept. The Jesuit fought the urge to collapse, the returning sound of Esaw's rattle just behind him, and stepped towards the beast. The demon turned and scattered back up the hill, vanishing into the darkness above. "*Abrenuntio,*" he sighed. "I renounce him."

Father Garner looked at Esaw and Mononcue, who now stood beside him. The medicine woman nodded at him. "Legion," Garner smiled dimly. "For we are many."

"And now?" asked Mononcue.

"The net grows smaller still," Esaw said. "Held on all sides now, and the dark will end. I cannot leave."

The devil stood at the top of the hill again, almost dancing within the trees shadows. "Then, we will finish this," Garner snarled at the thing and turned to complete the exorcism

Esaw grabbed his arm. "First . . ." her eyes narrowed, staring into the woods, watching the shadows beneath the trees.

Father Garner turned and said quietly, "The shadow people."

The forms were undeniably human, wraithlike wisps made of heads and shoulders and arms. The hips, however, ended in a cloud of blackness which rolled over what should have been legs in an undulating cloud of darkness. The shapes grew gradually, appearing slowly from behind pine trees and rising from under thick bushes. One moment, there was only a patch of forest gloom under a darkened sky; the next, the distinct and dreadful outline of a head and arms lifting from the shaded ground.

A dozen such shapes rose into the night, then twenty, then more. They floated slowly down the hillside towards them. The three formed a half circle, feet away from each other, the holy items of three tribes held before them in defense. Still above, Father Garner could see the devil orchestrating the nightmare with its own demonic dancing and shrieks.

Esaw turned her rattle differently than before, rolling it quickly between her two hands while creating wide circles that reached even past her head. The shadow shapes moved closer still.

Father Garner drew back his sword and prepared to strike. His knuckles turned white

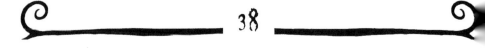

around the hilt, his knees shaking. He'd had little training in swordsmanship and even less in shadow people.

Something flicked behind him suddenly, and the priest turned to see light being drawn from his candle and Mononcue's lantern left just behind them. Some paranormal force of wind had drawn the glow from both in two long strands of light that expanded across the forest to reach them. The two glimmering beams curled finally over Esaw and then immersed into her rattle. The turtle shell shown brilliantly, glowing in a blinding light that made Garner turn away.

Esaw cast the rattle, dropping it towards the closest patch of shade. Light burst, again, from her talisman in a thin line of radiance, fed by the continuing strain still being pulled from the candle and torch. The beam struck the shadow person in the chest and the darkness vanished in an inhuman wail and a sudden spurt of black mist. She turned and cast her rattle again.

Father Garner pivoted himself and faced his own monsters. The darkness grew taller still, pulling in on the lower shadows of the close underbrush. They moved swiftly, floating towards him like unstoppable clouds of black. The head had become even more human and now showed the deep sockets of black eyes, the skin-stripped outline of its bone jaws and skull. "*Vade in pace!*" He swung his sword.

The blade slashed into the black thing as if passing through air, but it shrieked just the same as the darkness split in half and oozed in a dark mist back into the foggy ground. More dark shapes swarmed forward.

Garner took a defensive stance again and brought the sword up. From the corner of his eye, he saw more flashes of light and could make out Mononcue striking at the storming shapes with his bow.

Two more shadow creatures emerged from the darkness right before him and floated to either side of him. He started swinging God's blade again. And, again.

When they were done, the three stood together as before, looking up the hill at the creature. "Now?" Garner asked, breathing tiredly.

"End this," replied the Lenape medicine woman, her face streaked with perspiration and lined with pain. "I can keep the net, yes? But, only a little longer."

Mononcue scowled. "I will watch for more shadows." The Huron looked at his bow, wiped the black stain of night from its tip.

Garner nodded, and the two men watched as Esaw closed her eyes and started chanting in a language he recognized as similar to Lenape. The turtle-shell rattle had once again taken

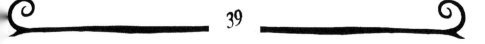

up its quiet and steady rhythm.

The priest stumbled to his own cloak and fell to his knees before the items there. He began murmuring the Litany of the Saints and opened one of the vials. Inside was holy water, and he splashed it towards the demon, sprinkling over the pines. When the vial was empty, he closed his eyes and finished the Litany. "Amen, Amen, Amen I say to you," he gasped and grabbed hold of the small bell.

"I sound the bell." Garner rang it three times, the tone low and ethereal. The creature shrieked once in response, overriding the bell's sad sound. Five times again, he rang. Then three more. "*In nominee Dei*, in the Name of God Almighty, I command you. End the killing and assault of these lands. You are banned for a thousand years."

The devil flapped its wings and tore up chunks of the earth, throwing dirt and shrubbery in a maniacal tantrum. Garner looked down at the book and the slip of paper he'd placed within. "LEGION" read the slip he'd written in the morning. "I close the book." He shut the old tome on the slip of paper, the demon's true name now sealed on all sides.

The creature fluttered, lifting in the dark morning's air, rising like some dark angel, like Lucifer in Starlight. Can it ever be truly saved, he wondered. "*In nominee Dei*, you shall not leave until you have sworn to uphold this oath!"

"Quickly," Esaw hissed beside him. "It is breaking. I can not . . ."

It has not agreed, Garner shuddered. It has not sworn.

The demon dropped back down to the earth, its eyes red and blazing in anger. Eyes that would never agree to his demands.

"It thinks it is caught until we free it," the Lenape woman said. "Quickly."

Father Garner tapped the relic around his neck. He thought of soldiers who would not relinquish and stared at the Leeds Devil again. "*In nominee Dei*, I command you. You are banned for a hundred years."

He felt the change immediately, darkness lifting from the forest. The shadows around the trees and underbrush pulling back. It had agreed to the altered terms.

Hands shaking, he picked up the lit candle. "I quench the candle," he whispered and blew it out at last. He jumped to his feet with his sword again, which he used to draw a pentagram in the air. "By the sign of Light," he concluded in Latin, "I seal this Sanctuary."

The devil shrieked once more and then lifted into the clearing sky, rising over the trees at last. Freed.

Garner knelt again in the sandy soil and pine needles to pray. Esaw and Mononcue approached, their eyes as weary and dark as his own, he supposed. They crouched beside him.
"The treaty?" Esaw asked.

"A hundred years," Garner replied.

She nodded and smiled tiredly.

He touched his fingers to the candle, the wick and wax still warm to the touch. "The demon will keep peace for a hundred years. After all," the priest added watching the strange spirit vanish again beneath the horizon and into the trees. "We now have its promise."

"I feel it," The magic woman said. "The forest feels it. I believe it is so."

"Do you?" the Huron asked the priest, his eyes sharp and probing.

Believe that it will keep its promise? Or believe that the Leeds child is savable? Either way, it didn't matter.

"*Credo*," Garner replied.

NOTES: The Leeds Devil is said to have been banished by "bell, book and candle," and that the exorcism rite lasted for a hundred years. There are Leeds Devil stories and sightings between 1740 and 1840, but the creature was noticeably much more reclusive and passive during this time. The people of the Pine Barrens grew nervous with the coming of 1840 and sightings increased again that same year. The Leni Lenape tribe (the Delaware) dwindled in numbers due to disease and English encroachment onto their lands, and members of the tribe moved reluctantly into the Pine Barrens as more English settlers arrived in America.

The Huron and other Eastern woodland Indians suffered similar fates. So, too, did the French, who lost Canada to the English at the end of the French and Indian War in 1763.

CAPTAIN DECATUR AND THE WIZARD
1809

The creature watched them from just above the jagged tree line, the setting sun glowing crimson behind its peculiar dark shape. It was larger than a man and had enormous wings spread wide that fluttered leisurely as it hovered in its spot. A giant bird of some kind, perhaps. But, a bird with a long tail swinging under its legs. A bird with arms? A dragon?

"What, in the name of God . . ." Stephen Decatur muttered, squinting hard. Though he was surrounded on all sides by his men, no one responded.

Seeing Decatur now, one might not have realized he'd been a celebrated naval lieutenant in the service of President Thomas Jefferson. Sweat dripped from his face, and hair and had stained his cotton shirt. His pants were dirty, too, from several days on the firing range. He'd been crouched over several eighteen-pound cannonballs, rolling each across the ground to judge which had the more perfect sphere, when he first saw the thing.

He stood slowly and, immediately, looked more like the naval hero he was. His exploits in Tripoli, recapturing, then burning an unsaveable USS *Philadelphia* promised a distinguished future. And, since the new Madison administration faced continued maritime problems with Britain, officers like Decatur were a high priority, as was America's naval preparedness.

Decatur's bearing appeared tall and straight, full of earned confidence that belied his thirty years of age and a personal strength that remained despite a long day's work over the blistering guns in the hot south Jersey sun. His nose and features were sharp and considered handsome, his eyes wide with focus and intelligence. He reached out a hand and one of his men instinctively handed Decatur his telescope. "Mr. Morris," he called the furnace master to his side. "Can you explain?"

Morris scratched his head. "Captain, I . . ."

In the focus of the telescope, the creature appeared even stranger. Decatur clearly saw what looked to be a reptilian tail hanging from the animal. Leathery wings. A face so hideous, the telescope actually wavered in his hands. "It is a demon," he declared. His grip tightened on the scope, but still the thing shook in his grasp, and Decatur lowered it quickly, cursing himself.

The hardened furnace master at his side swallowed once before speaking. "The Leeds Devil," Morris said, the words as strained and taut as his face. "A demon, indeed. It hunts our children."

"Midshipman Conly," Decatur ordered. "Load *that* cannon with *that* ball, if you please."

He pointed to one of the cannonballs he'd been evaluating. The ball was immediately loaded into the great gun's muzzle and rammed down onto the canvas bags of powder they'd set.

Decatur took a length of wire looped on his belt and jammed it through the cannon's touch-hole, piercing the canvas bag beneath. He then took one of the priming tubes, a reed filled with finely milled powder, and slid it down the powder charge, leaving a half-inch of reed sticking above the cannon. He grabbed a handful of pine needles from the ground and tossed them into the air, gauging the wind. He looked through his telescope again and slightly turned the elevating screw on the cannon, ordering the big gun shifted a half-inch to the right. He squinted down the barrel a final time and nodded.

"Fire, Mr. Lewitt," he said stepping aside and raising his telescope again.

The other men held hands to their ears and waited for the explosion as Lewitt took a glowing linstock from a protective barrel and reached across the gun's wheel to touch the fire to the fresh reed. A moment later, the cannon exploded in a booming fury and rolled back five feet, the air filling again with familiar, acrid smoke.

Decatur watched the extraordinary beast in his lens, growing ever more disturbed by the physical characteristics he'd begun to detail. The hair-spotted hide, the reptilian snout, the glowing eyes. He had to wait only a moment before the cannonball found its mark.

The shot had been dead on. Perfect. Later, Decatur would maintain he had not prepared a finer shot the entirety of his career. But, none of that mattered.

When the ball stuck the demon, none of the expected possible consequences occurred. The monster did not simply explode in a gory burst as many vessels and walls had done hundreds of times before. Nor did the force of the hurtling cannonball knock the demon back into the forest. Instead, the ball seemed to pass through the creature altogether. It hadn't missed. It had simply gone through and shot out the other side of the horror as if it were passing through. Through a ghost.

Talk broke out around him, the babble of shock and confusion. Decatur kept his scope lifted to see if the cannonball had indeed blown straight through the center of the beast, the damage so quick that the mortally-wounded thing didn't even know it yet. But, the telescope told another story. The creature looked the same as it had before, no damage at all. If anything, the demon seemed *more* alive, its tail twisting in the wind a bit more. And Decatur was half-convinced it was looking back directly at him.

"The wind must have took it," one of the men offered.

Decatur slowly lowered his telescope and half-heartedly turned to order another shot.

The monster moved then. Its wings flapped out in a broad, lazy, span and the creature lifted several feet into the sky, turning sidewise so that even from afar they could see its serpentine body and tail. It quickly dipped down again against the tree line, vanishing into the darkening pines.

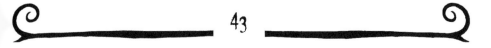

"It was the cannonball, sir," the furnace master said carefully.

"Your cannonballs are first-rate, Mr. Morris," Decatur laughed grimly. Buckets of water lay close by to cool the sweltering cannons, and Decatur leaned over one, scooping the water into his mouth and against his flushed face. "Would you like to tell me what this 'Leeds Devil' is, sir?" He stood, accepting a towel to dry his face and hands. "Or am I to infer that dragons are just something one gets use to whilst living in New Jersey?"

Decatur watched several looks pass between Mr. Morris and the other men on the furnace staff and waited. "A sort of legend we've got in these parts," the furnace master replied at last.

"The minotaur is a legend, Mr. Morris," Decatur replied. "*That* thing is something else entirely."

The furnace master just nodded.

"Perhaps we hit it, captain," Lewitt said. "It may have flown off only so far as to die."

Conly concurred quickly. "I took down a deer a week ago that run three miles with my shot straight through its heart. Sir."

"Indeed," Decatur watched his men warily and then looked back down the field towards the rest of the iron works. The Hanover plantation included one furnace, several forges, and a dozen charcoal pits to fuel the entire show. The village was comprised of the workers' homes, a sawmill and grist mill, a small general store, and a church that seconded as a schoolhouse. Decatur figured there were at least four hundred men within the plantation, a mixture of Irishmen, Negroes, Quakers, and Indians, most hired simply as lumbermen who provided timber for making the charcoal. A thousand acres of company woodland surrounded them completely on three sides, a thousand acres few had ever even seen, from what he understood.

"You've spotted this thing before?"

The furnace master shrugged. "Only once before, captain," he said. "Most here have never seen the creature. Perhaps the bigger cannons drew its attention."

"I want to find this thing," Decatur pronounced. "In just a month, the cannonballs produced here shall supply our operations. We have confirmed that a fitting product is produced here and will be essential for our ships of the line." He bowed to the furnace master, then refocused on the others. "I now wish to confirm that nothing shall interfere in the production of said product."

"Captain," the furnace master began. "I wouldn't—"

"Perhaps not," Decatur finished his thought. "But I must." He looked again into the darkening woods, the disappearing sun etching ever deeper shadows in the endless pinelands. "I wish to know its circumstance and its intentions. And, if either prove foul, we shall deal with the creature accordingly and swiftly. Mr. Lewitt, please inform the other Marines that we will set out first thing tomorrow morning."

"Yes, captain."

"Mr. Morris, I respectfully request one of your men as our guide, as I remain quite certain we'd be lost in this infinite forest without one." Decatur patted the heavy cannon beside him, the dark shadows of the tall pines now stretching over the long metal like black fingers. "The Leeds Devil," he tried the words again.

At dawn, Captain Stephen Decatur surveyed the mysterious Barrens from horseback with six of his own men and Caleb White, the young iron miner who'd been appointed as their escort. Each man had been supplied with musket, sidearm, and sabre.

They'd ridden slowly for an hour and now stood just beneath where they'd seen the creature to inspect the area for any signs of the beast's carcass, or prints of some kind or any indication that it had been hit at all. They'd found nothing. "It always flies off," Caleb White said quietly, as they saddled again.

"But," Decatur responded. "To what destination does it fly? Does this creature have a home?"

"Several, from what I've heard," the boy said, shrugging. "Comes and goes, goes and comes."

"Well, in this case, it flew south," Decatur said. "We'll follow its course." At that direction, he noticed the immediate change in the guide's face. "Mr. White?"

"There's . . . well, sir," the young man said, twisting his reins with sudden intensity.

Decatur rubbed his mare's neck and watched the young guide. "Speak freely, Mr. White," he said.

"They say there's a wizard who lives in those parts," White fairly blurted. "A whole settlement of witches, I've heard."

"A wizard." He turned to his own men who grinned at the boy's outburst, then sobered at Decatur's grim attention. "You've heard of this?" He asked looking back to the guide.

"Around the furnace, sir. The other men."

"More legends around the furnace," Decatur smiled. "Always surprising any work is done at all."

"Yes, sir."

"And what foul powers does *this* phantom of the pines have?" he asked.

White frowned. "Once the wizard and some of his posse was looking for work at one of the iron furnaces, Batsto I think, and when they told him no, he filled the furnaces with crows. Hundreds of them. Black and white ones. They just kind of appeared. And, as soon as he got

the job, they flew away again."

"Crows?"

"And once," White continued, genuine excitement warming him to his tale, "He came upon a six-mule team that couldn't get the wagon and its cargo over the hill. Munyhon, that's the name, just took the Leghorn rooster he was holding, tied it alone to the tongue of the wagon and said "Shoo!" That rooster had that wagon over the hill just like that.

"I see," Decatur pulled back on his horse. "Well, as we are properly equipped and trained to handle a, what shall I call it, a demon, dragon, a ghost? A simple wizard and his stout rooster should prove quite within our facilities."

"Yes, sir," the young man replied, and Decatur recognized the tone immediately as one he'd used himself many times before. It was the respectful tone of, "You're wrong."

They came upon the settlement several hours later. A mishmash of wood shacks with sod roofs. Maybe a dozen homes from what Decatur could see. The children and women had scurried back to the darkness of those same homes when they'd ridden up. Three bearded men with muskets met them at the top of the settlement.

The tallest spoke first, asking their business in a thick German accent. A Hessian, Decatur decided studying the man's manner, a mercenary soldier fighting for England during the War for Independence.

"I am Captain Stephen Decatur, a United States naval officer," he announced. "We have business in Hanover, where we were accosted by a creature most strange."

The men looked at each other. From their garb, and how the held their muskets, Decatur decided the others were not Hessian. "What do you want?" the man asked again.

"We found tracks a half mile that way," Decatur turned back the way they'd come. "Odd tracks. Not quite horse. Not quite bear." He looked at his own men. The tracks they'd found had scampered about a section of pineland just beside a small stream. The shredded remains of several fish had been found among the same marks.

"Back to Hanover," one of the men grunted. Decatur noticed the man had lifted his musket some.

"They're Tories, sir," Conly hissed quietly behind him.

"Yes, Mr. Conly," Decatur allowed. He knew that many of those who'd opposed the War for Independence, many of the most unrepentent Tories, had fled into the Pine Barrens to avoid persecution or death. It seemed both groups, the Tories and retired Hessian soldiers, had sought refuge in the boundless and bountiful pines. "But, that war is long over," Decatur con-

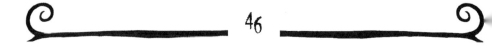

tinued, speaking low. "We have no complaint with these folk." He turned back to the settlers. "We have no quarrel here and will depart presently. We merely want to track down this monster, this 'Leeds Devil.'"

"And what will you do when you find him?" a new voice said from behind them.

Decatur turned again, half expecting that the monster itself was standing behind them. Instead, he saw a man.

Shorter in stature than most men Decatur had ever seen, the man's slender build and strong forearms and hands suggested he was used to working hard outdoors. A woodcutter, perhaps. He kept a short beard, peppered with grey and a wide hat stuffed with colorful feathers. In his left hand, a short cane made of dark hickory.

"Jerry Munyhon," their guide gasped.

The man nodded. Decatur turned back to the boy and saw a reverence in his eyes, an almost fear, that he'd not seen since he and several of his men had been once introduced to then-President Jefferson. He looked again at the new man. Jerry Munyhon, the wizard of the pine barrens.

"Sir," Decatur began, "I am—"

"I know who you are," the man said.

"We mean no trespass."

Munyhon smiled. "And yet you trespass."

Decatur's eyes hardened. "This land is owned by the Hanover Iron works, sir," he said.

"This land is owned . . ." Munyhon mimicked. "This land . . . ." He stepped closer, and Decatur got his first good look at the man's eyes. Intelligent, piercing eyes. Grey eyes that had seen much and also knew much. "This wood does not yet recognize other powers, Mr. Decatur. This wood does still recognize other powers. You best understand such a thing before you go wandering too far into it."

"Do you threaten us, sir?" Decatur glared at the man.

Munyhon laughed.

The captain noticed for the first time that the three villagers had vanished into their homes leaving Munyhon alone with seven armed trespassers.

"You're looking for the Leeds boy," Munyhon said.

"The demon," Decatur corrected him, having learned the evil history of the creature the night before. "Do you know where I might find it?"

Munyhon only smiled again.

"The iron master told us of an abandoned mill," Decatur said. "Perhaps two miles that way. Is that right?"

"You don't want to go there," Munyhon said, his smile fading. "I suggest you all just head back to your furnaces and cannons."

"Or?"

"Or," Munyhon considered. "He'll kill every one of you."

Decatur turned to his own men and then looked back at Munyhon. "Our conversation is at an end, sir," he said curtly. "Thank you for your time." He pulled his horse and started out of the settlement.

"I can't let you do that," Munyhon said behind him, and Decatur spun around to assure the man he hadn't the faintest care what the scruffy conjurer thought.

But, the "conjurer" had lifted his hand and cane, the movement both swift and easy. And, what he threw, if Munyhon had thrown anything at all, Decatur would never know. As soon as Munyhon's cane went up, several of Decatur's men at once dropped from their saddles to the ground. Pushed somehow by the motion of Munyhon's movement. Grunts filled the camp as several bodies hit the forest floor.

From the corner of his eye, Decatur saw the pistol rise. "No!" he shouted.

Lewitt's pistol fired with a crack and echo that filled the woods in a plume of smoke. Decatur's horse reared at the sound, and he pulled the animal back into line. "Hold your fire," he barked. "Hold your fire."

In front of him stood Jerry Munyhon. The tiny man held out his free hand as if offering an apple. Yet in the hand, he held only a round pellet. He rolled the bullet in his palm as if it were still hot.

"Blessed," the guide, White, gasped behind him.

"Impossible," Lewitt said, dropping the pistol limply to his side. "I hit him square."

"A trick," someone said. "They switched out our pellets at Hanover."

"You missed," one of the men tried.

"As I missed the demon?" Decatur asked, his eyes fully on the strange man before them.

Munyhon dropped the pellet onto the ground. "Captain Decatur," he said quietly, motioning for Decatur to follow him. "Would you care to speak in private prior to completing your duty?"

Decatur nodded and dismounted his horse. His men patted the dirt from their backs and bottoms and watched nervously as he followed the conjurer deeper into the village. Munyhon led him to one of the smaller cabins and opened the front door, allowing Decatur to enter first.

Decatur stepped into the dank cottage and waited quietly as Munyhon opened shutters and allowed light and fresh air to enter the cabin. "Your home?" he asked.

"At times," Munyhon replied. "At times. Whiskey?"

"Thank you, sir," Decatur accepted a cup half filled with a bitter swill that proved a distant cousin of whiskey at best. He coughed on the next sip.

Munyhon downed his own drink. "What is it you're searching for out here, Mr. Decatur?" he asked.

Decatur set his own drink aside. "I want to know how a cannonball passes straight through a flying monster," he said. "Now, I also want to know how a man catches bullets in his bare hands."

"Magic," Munyhon replied, filling his own cup again.

Decatur grunted.

"You do not believe?"

"I believe in what is real," Decatur replied. "The stars in the sky and the iron in the forges. The tides, my men. These things are true, they are either black or white, and I base my life upon them. They are real."

"Honor and duty," the haggard man countered. "Nationalism and faith. These things are true and you base your life upon them. They are ethereal, not real. Sometimes they are quite grey. Magical, yes? I told you these woods still recognize another power."

Decatur picked a glass ball off the table. It was the size of a small cannonball and had thick colored strings running through its hollowed center. "A magical ball, I presume" he said.

Munyhon nodded. "It is, indeed, called a witches' ball. For telling the future."

"Are you truly a sorcerer then?" Decatur asked.

"Who's to say what anyone truly is?" he asked thoughtfully. "Especially out here." Munyhon stepped closer, and Decatur fought the urge to retreat. "Hold the ball still," Munyhon said, "And let me take a look."

Decatur's eyes narrowed, but he kept the ball in his hand and held it out for Munyhon to look at it.

The wiry man stared into the glass for only a few moments, smiled briefly, and then nodded. "Where there is no honor," he said. "There is no grief."

"And what is that to mean, sir," Decatur snapped, stepping away from the wizard and replacing the glass ball onto the table.

Munyhon shrugged. "Perhaps nothing."

Swallowing hard, Decatur cooled his aggravation. "You wished to speak, Mr. Munyhon? I would hear you out."

"You shouldn't go up to that mill," Munyhon said.

"Then the creature does dwell there."

"At times," Munyhon said. "At times."

"Why do you not drive him out then? I can send for more men and—"

"Perhaps you've already forgotten the 'He will kill all of you' warning?" Munyhon smiled.

"I have not," Decatur replied. "But, neither will I be frightened away by old legends or 'monsters.'"

"And your men, captain? What of them?"

Decatur didn't care for the way Munyhon had said 'Captain' and recognized the implied barb, but replied anyway. "My men have followed me into battle against the Barbary pirates to retrieve a ship from a hundred murderous heathens. They will most certainly join me in this exploit."

"To kill the Leeds boy?"

"I told you, Mr. Munyhon. I've come only for answers. Where those answers direct my duty next, I can not say at this time. A predator of humanity? A misshapen animal? This Leeds Devil . . . I just want to know what it is."

Munyhon studied Decatur for a moment and then cast his eyes briefly to the witches ball on the table. Decatur began to speak, but cut his breath short as Munyhon waved his hand.

"Very well," Munyhon said, finishing his second drink and reaching for his cane. "Very well." He stood, eying Decatur with his sharp eyes. "Though I don't know how many answers you will find up there."

Decatur followed Munyhon from the cottage and marched at his heels into the woods. He patted both the pistol and sabre at his side and wondered briefly if he should include his men. He did not raise the question however. It seemed clear Munyhon would allow only him.

The discarded mill was another mile into the woods. It was an ancient and rotted structure, half collapsed into the stream it once bridged, half lost in shadow, though the late afternoon sun shot beams of sunlight through its cracked and broken form. A strange multicolored light swirled within.

"Who built this mill?" Decatur asked, surprised to hear his voice had grown hushed in the gloom of the half-light.

Munyon just shrugged.

Watching the mill, Decatur blinked, unnerved by the dance of light and shadow. "Doesn't the village fear the creature so close?"

"Yes," said Munyhon. "But, wise fear begets care. They do not disturb it, and he, for the most part, has not yet disturbed them."

"For the most part?"

"Livestock is taken."

"I see," Decatur said. "So, now what do you propose?"

"Go and seek your answers," Munyhon offered.

"What about you? What about the Devil?"

"Go on," Munyhon grinned, motioning for Decatur to go in himself. "Surely can't be worse than 'a hundred murderous pirates.'"

"Very well." Aware he was being needled, he scowled. "Very well indeed."

Stephen Decatur's steps towards the mill were careful and steady. Small twigs cracked under his boots as he walked into the long dark shadow of the mill. He unstrapped his pistol and peered inside.

The mill seemed empty, the light trickle of water reverberating up to its partially collapsed roof. Multihued lights, in tones of red, yellow, blue and green, played off the wood walls. He saw where the remains of some animal lay. He saw where several old chairs had been pushed aside, where leaves and pine needles had been bunched up in one corner of the hollow inside.

He saw where something large, something massive, had recently laid down to sleep.

Then, he saw the glass.

Hundreds of fragments of glass littered the floor. Thousands, perhaps. Different shapes and colors throughout the collection. And, the glass was not heaped in a meaningless pile. Nor was it spread haphazardly across the floor. No, Decatur decided. This glass, these treasures, had been laid out quite intentionally.

He found shapes within the glass montage, design. At first, he saw only patterns and shapes. Then, some of the shapes suggested forms he recognized. A woman's face, a deer, a house, the moon. Some of the images he could not make out, some quite repulsive and violent, others quite sad somehow.

As the sunlight spilled into the house, Decatur realized that it reflected off the same glass and it mirrored against the left wall of the mill in a dazzling display of color. He wondered how moonlight might play off the same art.

A presence behind him alerted him, and he whirled around, drawing his pistol.

It was Munyhon.

"What is this?" Decatur demanded, gesturing at the display. He stepped away from the glass, and holstered his gun. "He did this. Why is this here?"

The conjurer only shrugged again.

Decatur looked at the glass again and then up into the shadowed beams of the rotten structure surrounding them. "Woe to him who is alone," he quoted the Bible.

"Indeed," Munyhon smiled thinly from under his beard.

"You'd said these woods still recognized other powers," Decatur said and crouched down to inspect the glass more closely. Myriads of pictures, all carefully laid, intercut with shards of precious, vibrant color. Strangely affecting, the creature's dedication to his task. *Was such a thing possible?*

His glance swept outward. In the dust on the floorboards, he saw prints again. Prints he'd seen before. The prints of a dragon, or a demon. Perhaps of something more. "Something that wasn't quite black or white. Something in between. Something grey, I think you said."

"You finished here?" Munyhon asked. "It'll be dark soon and we best be getting back. Just in case."

"I wished to learn the creature's circumstance and intentions. I'm not sure . . ." Decatur shook his head. "I am finished here." He stood, straightened his vest, and followed Munyhon out of the mill into the dipping sunlight.

He looked at the mill again and then turned to take in the entire barrens, the darkening trees and endless brush surrounding him for a hundred miles in every direction. An uncharted and mystifying land half buried in legend. He turned to Munyhon.

"But," he added, "I should still very much like to meet your rooster, I think."

Munyhon laughed. "That, we can do Captain Decatur. That we can do."

NOTES: Stephen Decatur was already one of America's most distinguished naval officers when he met, and fired upon, the Jersey Devil. He later served in the War of 1812 and reached the rank of Commodore by 1814. He died in 1820, the result of a duel with Captain John Barron in which his honor directed Decatur to shoot his younger rival purposefully in the leg. The rival was directed differently. Jerry Munyhon, the Wizard of the Pines, is a true Barrens legend who purportedly lived from 1750-1865 conjuring the same feats, among many others, described in this tale.

UNDERGROUND
1858

There were five men in the posse. Each carried a rifle, and two aimed squat oil-fed lanterns to direct broad flushes of light though the dark pines. They also had the bloodhound.

The four, who'd come up through Maryland, had picked up a federal marshal in Camden. The enhanced gang now stood just outside Pasadena, a small and currently empty mining mill deep within the Pine Barrens. One of the original hunters called the others forward and pointed to where he'd found the tracks again, leading into the vacant mill. "Got the dirty brute now," he bragged over the light fall of rain. "He's holed up in there for certain."

Their quarry watched from the night-shadowed recess of one of the mine entrances. His breathing was rough and filled the dark tunnel along with the thudding of his own heart. He risked another look behind, deeper into the tunnel. The back of his shirt was sticky with dried sweat and wet from the rain, his fingers numb from the three-hour flight through the icy rain and dark pines, and he warmed them quietly with his breath.

Just a week before, he'd been Collin Adams, the respected senior carpenter of the Berkman plantation, one of Maryland's largest corn farms. Tonight, he was Collin Adams, escaped slave.

Two choices, he reckoned, trying to focus through a haze of exhaustion. The first was out the hole again and across almost a hundred yards of open field back into the woods. But, the five slave hunters had the place pretty well marked, and there was no way he'd get by undetected. Too tired to outrun five men and their dog, too tired to keep outrunning them at any rate, Collin grinned. It had been a harried coach ride from his hideaway in the basement of the Indian King Tavern in Haddonfield to Chatsworth, where they'd been stopped, and he'd gone on foot into the pines. His grin faded as he thought over the only remaining option.

The second choice meant going further down into the tunnel, deeper into the underground darkness, perhaps to find another way out, a way unguarded. But . . . he swallowed, shifting his eyes forward.

The voices of the posse grew closer still, and Collin flinched. The men approached the opening, their lantern lights already casting an orange glow across the wall beside him.

But there is something down there. Something evil. He'd heard its breathing. Even above his own, a deep rasping sound coming from further back in the tunnel. He'd distinctly heard its body shifting in the blackness. And he could manage all of that, convince himself it was some bear or wildcat that'd crawled down into the tunnel to get some rest—but, it was a feeling of pure evil that had floated up out of the darkness towards him, a tangible sense of dread and fury, that had rattled him so. There was something more than an animal down there.

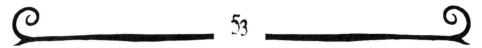

Something . . . something worse.

Still, he inched deeper into the darkness away from the bounty hunters' light. The decision, like so many before, had just been made for him.

"Just two ways out," one of the men laughed.

"Jeremy, Bernard, block the other tunnel," the boss, a man named Frank called out. "Where you gonna be, Lumley?"

"I'll keep watch," a newer voice answered, the voice Collin recognized as the federal marshal. "Can't be too careful out here."

"There are times, Marshal, I get the notion you don't take your sworn obligations quite so seriously."

"Well, you know how us 'Northerners' can be." The marshal smiled in his voice. "Seems a lot of running around in the woods and rain to find one man."

"Mr. Rudolph has sold said property," snorted Frank. "For a sum of five hundred dollars and is now unable to collect. I believe he, the fugitive slave law, and your boss, think its worth our running around."

The marshall breathed deeply. "I was only saying you can't be too careful, is all." He spit. "Especially out here."

Collin continued his retreat into the tunnel. The beam-supported roof only went four feet high, and so he crouched, backing away on his hands and feet like a Chesapeake frog. The walls to either side were wider, so that he could stretch out his arms and still not touch both of the dark walls. The hunters' lantern light suddenly flooded the top of the passage.

Whatever was behind him now stirred in the darkness. He heard it moving again, deep inside the tunnel, but already seeming too close. A heavy weight had unfolded itself like some hideous bloated monster in a child's nightmare, claws now scraping against the tunnel. Bits of dirt crumbled away from the walls in a jagged trickle.

His mother had told him stories about men who'd followed a porcupine or some such creature into its burrow and by and by found themselves in the underground village of the dead. The *mosima*, the abyss, the place where the shades and dead things dwelled.

Collin turned, the orange glow of the lantern above him washing over his back in a faint glow, and looked deeper into the tunnel. The light barely broke the darkness ahead of him, and his eyes struggled again to shake off the lantern's light and adjust to the undying darkness of the underground tunnel. The gloom stretched as far as he could see, further than he could imagine.

"Look there," a voice huffed from above and Collin's heart jumped a beat. "You can see where he's been sitting. Boots going down, we got him, but good."

"What are those there?" another voice asked. "Looks like horse tracks."

"Now, what kind of sense does that make?"

"Well, you're looking at the same thing I am! Ask him. He's got the funny look on his face."

The marshal's voice echoed down the tunnel. "I'm just cold is all."

"Forget it," someone stopped the discussion. "Send the dog in."

"Yes, boss." A dark shadow wavered faintly across the wall next to Collin, as one of the men stepped into the tunnel, and the dog's thunderous panting filled the passage. The creature shifted noisily behind him again, and Collin froze, trapped again between the two choices.

"Go on," the voice up top urged. From below, Collin could see the etched outline of his hunter crouched in the opening beside the dog. The animal had taken only a few steps into the tunnel, but now stood still, panting heavily just outside the darkness. "Go on!" the voice urged more angrily.

The dog took another few steps down the tunnel, then laid down flat on the ground, seemingly unwilling to press any further. Collin breathed out a silent sigh of relief and the dog's quiet whimpering trailed all the way down to him. "He won't go down," someone confirmed.

"Blasted hound," another shape forced its way into the tunnel and smacked at the dog's bottom. "Go on!" the leader shouted. A sharp bark filled the tunnel, followed by loud cursing. The two dark shapes collided suddenly, and the bloodhound pushed past the man back through the opening. More curses followed after its dark wagging tail.

"Should we go down?" a voice asked cautiously.

Frank grumbled just within the opening. "Looks like. Don't got all day to starve him out."

"Careful," the marshal warned, "That mine's closed out for good. Flooded or collapsed, no doubt."

The dark outline struggled back out of the opening, grumbling and cursing with each movement. "Jeremy!" the voice shouted up top. "You two get down that tunnel. Chase him on out this end!" He turned to the marshal and another bounty hunter. "Just like a 'possum," he cracked.

Collin Adams spun around again, thinking now of the other exit. If the two got behind him, he was caught for sure. His only hope was another way out, or maybe a place to hide them out.

He scrambled ahead on his hands and feet again, hunched over, the still air cold on his face. Light glowed for a moment to his left, and he realized for the first time where the second tunnel must be. He scooted faster down the tunnel, careful to stay quiet, and his eyes peered ahead, looking for the second tunnel—and looking for the thing at the end of the passage.

In the faint glow of the lantern coming down from the left, he saw now where the tunnel split off into different directions. The first led left, up around a bend to another opening and the lantern light grew brighter within. Voices spilled down the passage towards him. The hunters were indeed coming down after him. To his right was another passage, but it had been blocked off. Several boards crossed over the entrance, nailed against the supporting beams and someone had scrawled the word "DANGER" across one of the boards.

And just ahead, at the absolute end of the forbidding tunnel, Collin could make out another short passage that ended almost immediately in a collage of wood beams, dirt and more darkness. The tunnel had collapsed, and the lantern light from the left continued to weep down into the passage, filling in more of the detail before him. The ginger glow jumped and bounced along the dirt walls, casting strange shapes and shadows across his vision.

He squinted at the collapse, peering through the shivering shadows to make sense of the dirt piles, trying to figure out if there was a way to snake through. Total darkness filled the back corner of the collapse, and, yet, still something darker, some embodiment of night, filled most of the top passage. Maybe another tunnel. A way through to another exit and freedom.

Then he saw its eyes.

They were red tapered slits of fire burning at the far end of the main tunnel, blinking within that terrible night. Just above the eyes was the thing's mouth, its pointed fangs. The jaws gleamed, dripping and sharp in the dim promise of light coming towards them.

He now recognized that the darkness above the eyes was a living thing. It was the creature. The monster was upside down, hanging upended in the dark crevices of the collapsed tunnel. Its massive shape expanded to fill the passage wholly, and it moved towards him along the top like some monstrous spider.

Collin lunged towards the passage on his right and grabbed for one of the wooden boards to use as a weapon. The wood proved rotted and broke away easily in his hand. He pressed forward into the hoped-for safety of the darkness just within.

But, what if there were more monsters on the other side? What if that's the reason the passage had been blocked? What if the darkness on the other side was a den filled with a dozen of the same demon?

Collin thought briefly of calling out to the hunters for help, and turning himself in. Surely, it was better than being torn about by whatever monstrosity was moving towards him in the darkness. Surely . . . .

All fear is bondage, he thought suddenly. Something his sister had told him, and he drew another board aside.

On the other side came cooler air, the faint trickle of water. There, he thought, hopefully. There is the way out. Just behind, the dark thing loomed ever closer.

He bent around the broken board and slipped into the blocked passage. At his back, something heavy and alive scurried across the dirt top and hissed from the spot where the three passages met.

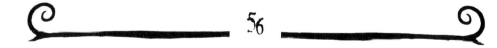

"What was that!" one of the bounty hunters gasped.

"Nothing, keep going," the second slave hunter told him.

Collin continued working through the opening. Pushing another board out of the way as quickly as he could, he made it through at last. Then, he sank into the chilled darkness on the other side. Cold water seeped into his worn boots, a thin trench of black water running up to the rotted boards.

"Heard something hiss," one man grumbled.

"That's just Adams. Come on."

The lantern's light touched the boards fully for the first time, the black shadows running lines across his face and hands. "Down here," a voice said. "There's a couple passages."

Collin Adams watched from just behind the boards, uncertain to move further into the hazardous tunnel just behind him, and even more terrified to return to the light. The two bounty hunters came out of their own tunnel stooped over with eyes wide. One held a shotgun, the other the lantern and a small pistol.

"Is that him there?" a voice asked.

"Sure," the other whispered. "Look, he . . . what is . . . ." His question cut off in a choked squeal, his last sound babbled and wet.

The thing moved with incredible speed, dropping from the ceiling just behind them like some demon wolf. For the first time, Collin saw its tail and the strange flaps running down its back.

He thought again of the tales he'd heard. Tales of the *madimo*, the 'monsters.' These were beings something less than human, somewhat more than animal. These creatures were said to be parts of the baboon and of the hyena. Long tails swishing, the sharp fangs hungry for man flesh. The bedtime stories told that witches and wizards sent such things out into the world to do their horrid biddings.

The lantern spilled to the ground amid odd screams and a first shotgun blast. The report filled the tunnels in an echoing blast that knocked Collin back into the second tunnel. Weird shadows moved across the walls and boards, shapes jumping in a frenzy of violence.

More shouts filled the passages now. Curses and hissing. Collin lurched to his knees again and fell towards the opening, arms grappling for purchase on the wet boards. Its tail was stretched out and covered in coarse black hair, a long donkey's tail, the flaps were wings of some kind, hairy dark wings. Shadows bounced up the passages outlining it, the body strangely human. It stood above the two men, its arms and legs thrashing in the gloom. Distorted snarls joined the men's high-pitched screams.

Collin looked again for a weapon, moved towards the opening. Bounty hunters or not, he thought, I can't just let it . . . . He moved back through the opening.

Gunfire filled the tunnel. And more screams from above. The others were coming down

the first tunnel now, and Collin fell back into his own passage, stumbling backwards again away from the commotion and hunters.

A shriek filled the cavern, a sound so awful, a roar so filled with dread and despair, Collin knew that way was no longer open to him, nor to any sane man. He moved back further into the tunnel.

Behind him, a lantern crashed to the floor and more screams filled the sudden darkness behind him. Other terrible sounds soon followed.

He ran. Collin staggered forward blindly, utter darkness filling the tunnel for the first time. He had never known such darkness. He was unsure if the next step would drop him in a well or into one of the creatures. He told himself there could be only one such creature in all the world. And told himself that again and again.

The water was up to his wrists and calves now. The corridor had flooded with rain water or river overflow. Either way, in a short time pushing deeper into the nothingness of the dark, he soon found himself crouched up to his knees in the dark water. For as far up as he could tell, the entire passage of the shaft was flooded. Fearing to look back again, Collin stumbled through the water, splashing in complete blackness, until he collapsed exhausted. The ground was slippery, covered in mud.

Quiet descended again as the screams and other gruesome sounds finally ended in the other passage. He breathed deeply once and got to his feet and hands again.

Moving through the tunnel was wet, but easy enough. Every now and then, he lost his footing and slipped harmlessly into the chilling water. The water tasted fresh, and he decided it was indeed rainfall, which meant that an opening, or at least several vents, existed some-where in the passage. If he found them, he told himself, then he could get out.

Up ahead was the faint hint of steady dripping, and he followed the sound. His head was pressed against the slippery top of the passage. The water, up now over his hip, left only a foot of air to breathe as he pushed down the corridor. His hands felt blindly in the darkness, try-ing to determine where the tunnel led as he moved forward.

He thudded into hard wood. His fingers clawed for an exit, an opening, and found noth-ing but a thin gap, barely enough for his arm to fit through.

Another collapse? After a few grim moments, he stopped, frowning. No. It was blocked. Collin sat cross-legged in the cold water, shivering in the dark. He had no choice, but to go back.

The sound of snapping wood suddenly echoed down the passage. The creature was now behind him. In his tunnel.

Collin shot to his knees again and began pushing through the dark opening, struggling to break through the tight crevice. His hands shot through a hole then, an open space higher than he'd felt before. He worked his head through the hole, sodden dirt casing his head. Ahead,

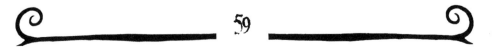

the pale hint of light.

He struggled harder, kicking against the muddy ground and squeezing beyond whatever opening he was passing through. His ribs seemed to crack and fold over on themselves as he squirmed and fought against the mud and jagged boards, the stench of rot filling his nose and mouth. He forced himself through and splashed into a short opening on the other side.

Breath escaped from him in ragged, panting gasps. His arms reached out into the darkness, and they touched the side walls, narrower now. He pressed forward.

He wondered dimly what the others were up to back at the plantation. Jackie and Otis, and old Scout. Probably hunched around the fire by now for sure, talking and eating Cookie Robin's fine apple cobbler. He snorted jadedly, hungry, a day now since his last bite to eat.

Something heavy splashed far behind him in the tunnel, and his trancelike crawl through the unseen muck quickened. The *madimo* was also still hungry. And, it knew the mine far better than he did.

The floor beneath his feet suddenly rose to a higher angle so that he had to crawl on his elbows and knees to work through the water. But, he was heading up. And, up meant out! Collin dragged along with his elbows pressed tightly to his sides, hands by his head, moving steadily higher, towards the light he'd half-imagined. The earth and water closed in around him.

"Steal away," he sang quietly, almost a whisper. "Steal away, steal away, ain't got long to stay here."

Scritch

". . . Steal away, steal away, ain't got long . . ."

scratch . . . schraa . . . schrii . . . .

Small red eyes gleamed just ahead.

"What?" He peered into the gloom.

scritch . . . srtittych . . . .

Something, just behind him now.

He tried to turn, but couldn't twist around in the narrow tunnel. More small eyes filled in the corridor just ahead. Through a rent in the tunnel's roof moonlight flooded the passage, blue and dreamlike, and he saw the first yellow hint of teeth. As his eyes adjusted to the growing glow of light ahead, he came to see. The tunnel was filled with rats.

At first, he could only stare in amazement as the mass of small, hairy, bodies quivered just in front of him. Cold water rushed under his mud-caked belly and traced a flood of rain-water into the tunnel. He felt the wetness run from his waist up to his back now. The water was rising.

The space ahead seemed narrower still, the dirt walls collapsed and spilled into the passage. The water high and rushing down towards him. Soon, the entire passage would be filled. *I'm going to drown,* he realized. Laughter bubbled up inside him, the choke of despair filling his ears.

"*And Moses stretched out his hand over the sea,*" he breathed, "*And the Lord caused the sea to go back.*"

He dropped his face into the cold water, felt its slow current running across his skin. Collin closed his eyes, and gave himself for a moment completely to the darkness—the rat-littered darkness. Just like one of the plagues, he thought. A plague of Egypt . . . .

Collin breathed deeply through his nose and, then, slowly lifted his head again into the black tunnel.

"The rats!" The laughter was wrung from him in short, explosive bursts. "Of course." The water had risen over his shoulders now. "Rats know where, where to get out." *The only question, now, is will I be able to follow?*

He grit his teeth and, with clenched fingers, inched forward down the narrow tunnel. The tiny eyes dodged around and eventually disappeared behind a corner to the right. A sharp board dug into his shoulder, a piece of collapsed tunnel.

Collin followed just behind as the troop of rodents continued fleeing away from the rising water. The passage continued at an angle, leading still upward.

He thought about his dream of a carpenter's shop in Canada, the one that would have a swinging sign over the front door and the woodcuts on the walls. He'd probably have to apprentice for a few years first, of course, but in time, he'd have a few clients of his own. Folks always needed chairs, cabinets, tables. As he crawled through the constricting muck, he imagined again the special tables and chairs he would make, the kind never before seen north of the Chesapeake Bay.

The rats scurried ahead, stopping periodically to see if they were still being followed by the strange man in the water, the man literally pulling himself from the underworld. Several more rats swam past him, keeping their heads just above the water as small, hairy bodies pressed against him, scratching as they went.

One large rat crept onto his back and sprang to safety from his shoulder. Collin stifled an instinctive scream and pressed forward.

The tiny black shadows scampered down a left passage, and he dragged behind, following as the narrow tunnel continued upwards. His hands dug now through the slop, pushing the dirt away to move forward.

Just ahead, the strange light glimmered brighter.

He pushed forward, every muscle in his numb body working towards crawling forward, pushing through the constricted passage. The water flushed into his face, and he choked on it as it poured down the tunnel towards him.

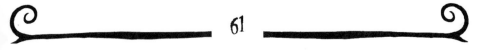

He heard the heavy, dragging sounds again behind him—close, only as far as when he first found the rats' nest. The *madimo* was coming.

An image of the beast filled his mind again, the pigskin wings and fiery eyes like torchlight, and he chased it away as best he could, focusing only on the next handful of dirt, the next handful of dirt, the next . . . .

Ahead, he saw the boards for the first time. Sharp black shadows crossing over the muck and gloom, blocking the full glory of the light beyond. It was indeed the way out, and he shook with satisfaction as he watched the last black shape of a rat slip through and into the woods.

Water teemed over the boards, splashing his face and hands as he pulled at the planks. The wood held against his weak pulls, so he now punched out at them. His carpenter hands were tough and strong, but he was so very tired, so very cold.

A screech filled the tunnel behind him. The same horrible cry from before, and he punched the board again with his fist.

The wood splintered, but he pounded it again. His knuckles split open, and dirt spilled atop his head. He squirmed forward and managed to push one board aside. Water rolled freely through the opening, and he sucked joyfully at the air just inches away. Behind him, the tunnel had surely filled with water.

Could the *madimo* breath water, he wondered, as another board broke away, and he wriggled through the opening. The splintered wood cut into his shoulders and hip as he slid at last into the open air of night.

Collin Adams lay on the ground, coated in a thin layer of mud, wet and shivering. He tasted the dirt in his mouth still, still felt the cold touch of the dark water, the colder touch of the darkness within the mine. His dazed and tired eyes looked up at the stars above, the blue light from the moon herself touching his face fully at last.

"Give me your hand," a voice said.

He noticed the shape beside him for the first time. A shadowed form leaned forward and held out its arm.

Collin lay still, and the shadow's hand stretched closer towards his. He took it and felt himself lifted to his feet. He stumbled, and the strong grip of the other held him steady against the feeling that he might collapse.

"You okay?" the voice said. He recognized it, finally, as the voice of the federal marshal. The bloodhound cowered at the marshal's boots.

"Those men," Collin said huskily looking at the dog, his voice a mere whisper, "they . . ." he caught his thoughts. "There's something down there," he said at last.

The marshal looked across the camp. "It took off that way," he said. "Saw it go. You must be Adams," he said simply.

"Yes, sir. Collin Adams."

"A carpenter or something, is that right?"

"Yes, sir." Collin breathed deeply.

The marshal studied him for awhile, rubbing his bearded chin and watching him shiver in the moonlight. Finally, he spoke. "In Whiting, there's a place called Gregor's farm I hear." Marshal Lumley looked down at his boots. "Keeps his hitch post lit most nights."

"I understand," Collin replied carefully.

The marshal reached down and rubbed the dog's neck. "Just follow that one," the marshal pointed up to the stars. "February," he grunted. "Should take you straight through."

"The north star," Collin confirmed. "The drinking gourd."

The marshal nodded.

"Sir. What about . . ." Collin stopped. "What was that thing?"

Marshal Lumley looked around the woods one more time and sighed heavily. "Be careful, Mr. Adams" he cautioned, turning away. "Can't be too careful out here, I'm told."

Collin watched him go until the marshal and dog had vanished completely into the pines.

Then, he marked his star again and started walking.

NOTES: New Jersey, just above the slave states of Maryland and Virginia, and populated with numerous abolitionist Quakers, played an important role in the Underground Railroad, a series of safe homes, farms and taverns for runaway slaves that ranged up through the North, all the way to Canada. A lit hitch light often identified a safe house. Haddonfield's Indian King Tavern (restored and active today) served as one of the many havens along the way. The Compromise of 1850 required Northern marshals and officials to intensify their help for southern posse's in the capture of escaped slaves. Ultimately, the requirement gave many Northern officials and people their first real look at the slave trade, and these more common Northerners soon joined the abolitionist cause. The Civil War began in April 1861. The setting and tunnels described are based on Pasadena, New Jersey, a small town in the center of the Pine Barrens built in the 18th century.

DEADLINES
1909

SUNDAY, JANUARY 17

The winter winds tapped at her window like tiny bone fingers, a crisp patter of icy snow blowing against the pane. Norma Wister shivered in the darkness beside her husband, the blankets and quilt curled carefully under her toes and up to her chin. She rolled to her side and sighed, unable to sleep, and thinking about the impending hassle of the snow-covered morning.

Something clattered above her again, the snow storm blowing a neighbor's shutter or broken tree limb across the roof. The sound scraped across the ceiling, rhythmic and slow, almost like steps. Like some animal slowly walking across the snow-covered roof. She stilled her breathing and listened, telling herself it was only the wind.

She nudged her husband, but knew he would sleep until morning unless the roof blew off entirely. And, even then, she wondered. She sat up straight in the bed and listened again. *Only the wind.* A wind that carried a low growl and now tapped rhythmically at her window in a slow, playful tempo.

Norma swung her legs off the side of the bed, her stocking feet hitting the cold wood floor, and stared at the window fully. Through a crack in the sash, she could see the snow sticking in wet drops against the pane and falling in the moon-tinted darkness behind it. There were more scuffing sounds from above, muted footfalls and something dragging across the roof away from the window.

The prancing and pawing of each little hoof. She thought of the popular children's book, *A Visit from Saint Nicholas* and chuckled gruffly. She wondered tiredly if the "Jolly Old Elf" had simply fallen behind schedule and then moved towards the window. No good letting some raccoon tear up the roof and ruin what might be left of a terrible night's rest.

Norma pulled the sash aside and wrestled the window up, shuddering before the cold air. Her husband stirred behind her, rolling away from the wind into the blankets, as she risked her head outside into the snowfall. The wet drops tickled her face, and she looked up and down the snow-covered street. Certainly, something magical about a world covered in fresh snow, she thought, leaning out the window to get a better look up the roof. It wouldn't have surprised her at all if Saint Nick, and his tiny reindeer, were there to greet her.

The hand that grabbed her from above was skeletal and long and wrapped completely around her face, the palm resting on the back of her head. Norma Wister screamed into cold knobby fingers, her shriek lost in the suddenly howling winds. The sting of sharp claws sunk into her chin and cheek, and she felt herself being lifted into the winter night.

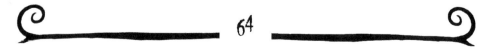

64

It wasn't Saint Nick.

MONDAY, JANUARY 18

The morgue was dark and forbidding, a permanent fire hazard stacked to the ceiling with dust-laden books, catalogues, maps, and more than ten years of clippings. Owen Henneberger stood against a small desk in the back corner of the room while his boss randomly rifled through one of the shelves. The boy, Howard, worked at another shelf behind him, carefully stacking photograph cuts and galleys of previous issues. "A monument to lost motion and inefficiency," the editor grumbled to himself.

"Sir," Owen said carefully. "Might I—"

"I suppose you've heard," the editor turned to Owen. "About this 'What-Is-It' creature everyone's talking about?"

"Yes, sir," he replied. There'd been some gossip out of Burlington and Woodbury. Even from Bristol, just over the river. Something about strange tracks in the snow, hoof prints as if the animal walked on only two legs. Several had heard the creature's call, a high-pitched shriek, and a few claimed to have actually seen the beast. A competitor, the *Camden Courier*, had already run a full story with the headlines, "Strange Animal Makes Excitement" and "Mysterious Attack Upon Milk Dealer in Mt. Ephraim Barn."

"What do you make of it all?" His boss stepped away from the shelf and stood before Owen now.

"I don't . . . well, it could—"

"It's the Leeds Devil, sir," Howard spoke out. "Isn't that right, Mr. Henneberger?"

The editor looked at the boy and smiled indulgently. Howard was a pale, thin lad no more then ten who hovered about the newspaper morgue and, for a few cents a week, ran small errands for the other reporters. He turned back to his morgue clerk. "Mr. Henneberger?"

"The descriptions are similar, sir. The tracks and horse face. I suppose — "

"That's fine, that's fine," the editor held up his hands to stop him. "The men upstairs reminded me you were interested in such things." He smiled again and picked the copy of *Argosy* off Henneberger's table. "Monsters and 'Men from Mars,' right?" Before Owen could respond, the editor finished his task. "Here's the matter. I don't have enough real writers to manage this hogwash at the moment. But, your obituary and fill-in work is certainly passable, and I feel confident this rat's nest can live without you for a few hours."

"Yes, sir."

"Thousand words, on my desk by four. We're already a day behind on it. The *Philadelphia Bulletin* ran this morning with it." And the *Camden Telegram* too, Owen thought but caught the words. "Witness reports," the editor was explaining. "Talk to Robbie, he knows a lot of the police." He stepped back from the desk, his eyes roaming over the room again with aversion. "Have fun with it, Mr. Henneberger," he said, stepping from the room. "Maybe you'll find one of those monsters you're so interested in."

"Yes, sir," he replied. "Thank you, sir."

TUESDAY, JANUARY 19

John Kelly thought it was some kind of monkey at first, the way the shadowed thing leapt out of the darkness and dropped onto the back platform of the trolley. A hairy chimp with a long tail that had escaped from one of the zoos. Then, he saw its wings. And, though he'd read his daughter's *The Wonderful Wizard of Oz* a dozen times before, Mr. Baum had never mentioned the jagged fangs, and John had certainly left his magical Gold Cap at home.

The trip to Clementon had been empty and quiet, and several passengers napped as the trolley moved slowly down the slush-covered road. It was late, the afternoon sun having already fallen behind the looming snow clouds. John had sat towards the back of the trolley. He'd stared absently out the window for most of the trip at the snow-covered trees and homes along the road, the day's newspaper laid flat in his lap. More on the blizzard. President-elect Taft was sailing to Panama. Several fires in town. And, strange animal tracks found in Collingswood and Haddonfield. A posse of hunters tracked the mysterious beast, "looked like a small cow" one woman claimed, and concluded it was a deer.

But what John Kelly was looking at now was no deer. It was no monkey either, flying or otherwise. The thing scurrying up to the top of the trolley, the thing that had literally made the car jump with its weight, was something else all together. He watched its tail, a reptilian tentacle sprinkled with bristly hair, slither up the back of the trolley and out of sight. Something moved just behind him now, and he turned around in time to see it.

A wet dark snout pressed against the glass, and its hot breath fogged just above the nose. He realized the thing was upside down, clinging to the top of the trolley, and looking in at them. The eyes at the bottom gleamed red and bright. The color of blood.

John screamed, and the terrible eyes, eyes far too human and intelligent, flashed back at him. Angry. Lost. Then the gaze dimmed, dropping away from the trolley within a black shadow that bounced off of the street and into the night. John made a strange sound, and the newspaper spilled from his lap as he staggered to the back of the trolley. Others in the car had turned lazily to see him, wondering what all the fuss was about.

Outside, the thing moved quickly away from them, hopping almost, down the street. One moment, the setting sun glowed orange off its winged back, and then it vanished completely into the darkness.

"A deer," he chuckled after the vanishing shape. Then, John's legs gave out, and only the dropped newspaper was there to break his fall.

WEDNESDAY, JANUARY 20

"The mysterious animal jumped on the rear platform, terrorized passengers and rang up sixty-five fares before disappearing in a luminous trail." Owen stopped reading and put the morning's paper back down on the desk.

"So?" The boss blinked, his eyes never leaving the page he was editing.

"And *rang up sixty-five fares* before disappearing?" His words came out in a gasp.

"Funny, huh?"

Owen rubbed his forehead. "Sir, this creature is—"

"Henneberger," the editor's voice was warning, but he still hadn't looked up from his desk. "Your work was fine. We just wanted to make it a little more . . . fun. So I had Welty touch it up a bit."

Owen warily dropped his finger on the illustration that had run with the article. "And the picture?" He couldn't bring himself to actually look at it again.

"Enchanting, isn't it? Fergusson did that from your description."

"Sir," he sighed, "It's wearing a top hat and smoking a cigar."

"It's still got the tail and wings."

He tapped the picture again. "What, in anything I submitted, would impart to you or Ferguson this image?"

"It's a devil or something, right? Mischievous. Carefree. Like a wandering scamp."

"No, sir," Owen groaned. "Not at all."

"The other newspapers are doing the exact same look. Henneberger, in case you haven't noticed, most everyone who doesn't live in a cave is treating this whole thing as a big joke."

"Not the witnesses I've interviewed."

"Drunks and loonies, all of them. I mean, come on. The creature's prints change size? A foot long and hooved in one yard, clawed and only inches long in another? It looks like an owl, donkey, some poor fellow's mother-in-law. Are you kidding? I told you, we needed to have some fun with this."

Owen breathed deeply and recollected himself. "Sir, what if we became the one paper who showed the beast for what it really was? Exposed the danger of it, the *horror* of the thing. Its murderous history."

"That's what the pulps and dime novels are for. We're a newspaper, Mr. Henneberger."

"But, you even cut out the part about Mother Leeds and the exorcism. That *is* the story, that's the news!"

"Who's ever heard of Mother Leeds?" the editor replied, looking up and setting the blue marked paper aside. "This is bigger than the Pines, Henneberger. It's the 'Jersey Devil' now."

"Fine. Then, at least call it that," Owen sighed, "The article names it only a What-Is-It or a flying kangaroo. The *Paterson Evening News* went so far as to call it a vampire!"

"A vampire," The editor nodded, thinking. "I like that."

"Sir, it's not—"

"Tell our readers what its called and bore them with some Pine Rat tale about a demon baby, and this story is done in one day. Decent folk aren't going to read such claptrap. But, if we can keep the people playfully guessing what it is, maybe even run a contest to name th thing. Then, we've got a story with some legs, maybe run for a week if we're lucky." He grabbed another article to edit. "You let me worry about selling newspapers, Mr. Henneberger. You just go out and drum me up some more witnesses. Good work."

"Yes, sir," Owen replied, turning to leave. "Thank you, sir."

"And, Henneberger," he called out behind him. "If you can do anything with the vampire angle, do it. People are mad for vampires."

THURSDAY, JANUARY 21

They worked through the files together well into the night. The morgue was cold, the new furnace unable to keep up with the frosty winter. The boy had his own pile of older clippings and a stack of source books, Owen sat with the past week's papers from a dozen different publishers spread out before him in a seemingly haphazard pile.

Tracks had appeared in Camden and Moorestown. Tracks that ended at bare walls and passed straight through, or over, tall fences. Collingwood, Mount Holly, and Riverside too, and strange cries were heard at all hours of the night. Several persons, respected citizens of various trades, claimed to have seen the beast directly. The descriptions varied, one witness said was a kangaroo with wings, another put it as a large dog that walked on its hind legs. It ran, hopped, it limped, it flew across open fields and perched in window sills, it rode a bike. Some said it was seven feet high, other put it at no more than three feet. The first time someone claimed to have killed the creature, it was discovered they'd only shot an opossum.

But Owen read other pieces too, something he'd done for years, the news within the news. While most morgue clerks had been assigned the job by an editor hoping they would quit, he volunteered for the job and never complained once. Looking for patterns and coincidence, the stories where there wasn't any. Possible clues to some larger story being told. He read about several elderly folk who'd died in their sleep, and middle-aged men and women who'd died heart failure, regrettable victims of the blizzard it was reported. Strain from the snow, the cold. How else to explain it? And he read of dog attacks, a man mauled so badly, he had not yet woken in the hospital. No witnesses, but everyone assumed it was one of the wild dogs that'd been coming up out of Cumberland. What else could it be?

"How's it coming?" he asked Howard.

"I don't know," the boy admitted, looking up from his work. "I've marked all the months with unexplained attacks and stolen pigs and the like. Any unexplained murders or disappearances." He'd charted the stories over various five year periods, running through back-page reports on Burlington and a small collection of law-enforcement correspondence going back to 1850. Looking for peaks in the violence, the bigger picture within the news.

"That's fine," Owen said. The Pineys believed the creature appeared more frequently just before a war. Agitated by the impending violence, or perhaps attracted to it. *Was the creature's sudden and volatile appearance some foreboding warning of a tragedy to come, some war on the horizon? And, if so, why had it reacted with such fervor this time?*

Owen slumped in his chair. Even if they found a provable pattern, what would his editor do with that story? He grabbed hold of a newspaper. "Remember the dentist we interviewed?"

"Absolutely," the boy replied. "He was still shaking during the interview."

Henneberger pushed his glasses back into place and read. "Dr. Alex Drews . . . the what-is-it perched on his window with an exposed sharp tooth very much out of repair. When the good doctor acted to help the mysterious beast and its unfortunate toothache, it flew away."

"A tooth ache," The boy shook his head.

"Look at the illustration." The hat and cigar were gone and the creature had the definite face of a horse finally, but now it was smiling with a big-toothed smirk. Grinning like a playful idiot. "Westville."

Owen put another dot on his map, a layout of New Jersey he'd made marking the times and exact location of sightings he believed to be legitimate. It was getting harder to know for sure as more and more people were jumping on the story. More witnesses each day. Was the creature getting more brazen or was every owl, opossum and dog being thought of as the Demon from the Pines.

At least, the paper had liked the map idea, and, only adding a picture of a bat in the left corner, printed Owen's drawing exactly.

He looked down at the map again, studying the jagged lines of the creature's travels for the hundredth time. He drew another line. "There," he said, pointing.

FRIDAY, JANUARY 22

The mounted policeman did not stop when Owen tried to wave him down. Instead, the officer hunched low against the cold flurry, his dark coat pulled high and close, as his horse simply galloped past and then vanished into the falling snow and darkness. Owen blew into his hands and rolled his shoulders hoping to shake off the bitter night's chill. The freezing wind swept down the West Collingswood street towards them, icy and harsh against his face, coating his glasses in frost.

Piercing, biting, cutting, sharp, Owen thought. These are the words of winter.

Howard stood beside him, chin to chest, arms wrapped tight against the same bleak elements. It had been a long night, but they were close.

They heard shouts again, faint echoes up the deserted street, and started jogging towards the muffled commotion. Closer to it.

Something was loose in Collingswood, something that walked like a man but looked like a kangaroo with a long neck. A vampire, perhaps, or a *Jabberwock*. Whatever some fool wanted to call it, it was stalking the city.

Owen jogged awkwardly, the cobblestone uneven under the snow and slick with an undercoat of ice. He passed several stores and a narrow alley. The boy ran just behind, panting. The shouts grew clearer.

A pistol fired, and Owen slid to a stop.

"Was that gunfire?" Howard panted, behind him.

The street ended at another cobblestone road leading right and left. Owen looked both directions and saw a small crowd gathering down the right street. Several hunched shapes rumbled past them in the snow towards the small crowd. "They shot it," one shouted raucously at Owen. "They shot the vampire."

"Come on," Owen grabbed the sleeve of Howard's jacket and pulled him back up the street they'd just come down. "That alley we passed . . ." he took a needed breath.

They stepped into the dim alleyway and angled past several trash bins and crates as the wind whistled strangely up the lane in a high mournful sound. The snow trickled down slowly, edging through the narrow space between the two blocks. Owen saw where the alley ended, a flash of light reflected off the snow, and he pressed forward. They stepped out onto a main street again. To their left, Owen could hear the others talking excitedly.

But, something else caught his eye just across the street from them. Some dark shape that moved in the shadows of the continuing alleyway. Owen stumbled towards it.

There were faint tracks in the snow, cloven footsteps already vanishing under the storm. And, dark stains, droplets of blood trailed deeper into the shadows. Owen and Howard moved slowly into the darkness.

The alley ended against a tall red-brick wall, and the Leeds Devil stood before it, half lost

in the back shadows.

Its horrible shape stretched up towards the moonlight, one arm reaching towards the ghostly light above them. Owen gawked at the monster, simply watching it. Reading it.

Piercing, biting, cutting, sharp, he thought again. These are the words of winter.

Then it turned and looked at them both. The red eyes flickered for an instant and then shined black. Empty black orbs blacker than ink. Dark and infinite.

Owen Henneberger screamed.

SATURDAY, JANUARY 23

"That's it?" the editor grumbled. "That's all you got? 'Police shoot at mysterious creature. What-Is-It presumed dead or wounded.' You two nitwits were there, for the love of Pete. I was hoping for a little more of the chase and shooting."

"Didn't see much," Owen replied flatly, then added, "Fergusson did the illustration." It showed a kangaroo-like character wearing mittens, a huge frown and a massive bandage wrapped around its head.

The editor glared at him, then smiled thinly. "Now, why do I get the feeling you're pulling my chain, Mr. Henneberger? That I'm not getting the full story."

Owen thought of the story Howard had written and left on his desk. Just under three thousand words typed out carefully on the busted Remington in the basement. Eerie and clever, the boy's words filled with the courage and promise of a future writer. The tale was set in New Orleans and the creature was something older and darker than what they had seen and yet . . . .

"What story would you want, sir?" he asked. "That we saw the monster, and it was evil incarnate, something not of this world? That its cruel eyes were literally filled with entire worlds of murder and suffering? That death itself seemed a better option than facing that terror for just another single moment?" He shuddered. "You wouldn't run a story like that, would you?"

"No, Henneberger, I would not." The editor rose from his chair. "That kind of talk, or story, that kind of *thing* you're clearly so fond of, has got no place among civilized people." The editor shook his head angrily. "Not in my paper. Not in *this* world."

Owen Henneberger stared out the window and watched the buildings across the street. The melting snow pooled in the cobblestone streets in black pools, pools dark and infinite. He looked at his editor.

"I couldn't agree with you more, sir," he said.

NOTES: In 1909, the Leeds Devil, or at least the idea of him, left the Pine Barrens for a brief visit to the big cities of Southern Jersey. Naturally, he became an instant celebrity and throughout the week, dozens of newspapers in Philadelphia and New Jersey ran with the story of his escapades and sightings. Though the Leeds Devil had been portrayed as a fearsome and vicious demon for more than one hundred years, the media portrayed him as a comical figure and gave him such names as *Kingowing, Woozlebug,* and *Asertoraskidimundikins,* (along with those mentioned in this tale), and then put him in topcoats or with silly expressions on his face. This general caricature is still the most prevalent today for merchandise (e.g.: t-shirts, PlayStation games, hockey mascots, postcards, etc.). His, so far, rare appearances in creative media, Hollywood and TV, naturally stick with the more fearsome and vicious demon manifestation.

CAUGHT!
1913

He breathlessly dropped the coins on the table, ten pennies to meet the very devil himself. And ten more for Ruby Miller's ticket. Oh, he beamed, how she will yelp with glorious fright when she sees the beast. Its red wicked eyes and razor-sharp teeth, its demonic wings. She will surely fall straight away into my arms. He smiled roguishly. Thank goodness they'd finally caught that wonderful Leed's Devil.

"And thank you, too, sir," the ticket seller said, scooping up the change. "Always wise to keep a brave man at hand, miss," he smiled at Ruby.

Arthur Pratt nodded back, grateful for both the man's crafty compliment and the sudden weight of Ruby's hand against his own arm. "Direct through those doors," the ticket seller said, winking at him. "The show's about to start."

Arthur pushed the tent flaps aside and stepped cheerfully into the darkness. Ruby followed closely behind, her hand still clinging to his arm for direction. Lantern light spilled through the walls, peculiar shadows moving against the canvas like black ghosts.

In the tent, a small crowd of maybe two dozen had already taken their seats, but there were two vacant chairs just to the right of the curtained stage. Arthur moved quickly for those, pulling Ruby behind him. "Arthur," she whispered urgently over the soft murmurings of the crowd. He found her voice a wonderful blend of alarm and melody. "I really don't—"

"Please, now, Ruby," he replied with calm authority. He even took the liberty to pat her hand, aware of her suddenly wide eyes and nervous mouth. He looked around the dim tent at the rest of the audience and the mysterious curtain before them. "You said you wanted to see it too," he urged. "Imagine, a real live monster."

"Yes," she managed. "Yes, I did say that."

The lights dimmed even more, if such a thing were possible, and their host stepped from behind the shadowed curtains into the room. He wore a black suit and a short rimmed hat and stood at attention, waiting for absolute silence to fill the tent.

"Good evening to all here," he said easily with a short bow. "My name is Stephen Compton, and I will be your host this night. I will lead you down dark paths towards something darker still, something more sinister than has ever been seen by man. Before we commence on our astounding journey, however, I am required by law to now warn you that you will hear and see things tonight that will shock and horrify you. The capture of this beast was a ghastly and terrifying adventure whose retelling has brought grown men to tears on many occasion. And to look upon the horror, the very devil itself . . . well . . . ." He glanced back uncertainly at the curtain behind him. "That is something else all together."

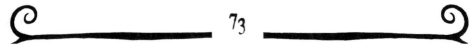

Ruby leaned into Arthur's side, her shoulder rubbing against his jacket. That's the ticket, he thought.

"At this time, anyone who wishes to leave the journey may do so. We will provide a complete refund to any who wish not to go any further tonight." His eyes roamed over the room for only an instant. "Very well, then. Let us begin."

Arthur turned to smile encouragingly and squeezed Ruby's hand. She scooted closer.

"You may already well know the tragic and horrifying tale of the Leeds Devil," Compton began. "The thirteenth child of a wicked woman, cursed from birth to become a monstrous demon. It is told that the night it was born, the creature killed, murdered, its own family." Several women shook their heads, but Ruby remained still beside him. "Afterwards," he continued, "when it had broken free into the ancient woods, not so quite far from this very town, it needed to feed. Livestock at first, but then babies began to vanish from their cribs. Small children never made it home. They hunted it, of course, and even attempted an exorcism once, but nothing worked against the horrid monster. And, for more than a hundred years, it has terrorized, and, I apologize to the ladies and children in the audience, fed upon, the fine citizens of this great Garden State." He lowered his head solemnly for a moment and then looked up into the crowd again proudly. "That is, of course, until we caught the wretched devil."

The crowd murmured its approval.

"But, I've gotten quite ahead of myself," he bowed theatrically in apology. At that moment, another man appeared at the front of the room. He wore a leather vest and a pair of scarlet pants. "I introduce to you Herr Ronald M. Shottelburg, one of the world's most celebrated and renowned huntsmen. From the darkest shores of Africa to the highest peaks of the Orient, Herr Shottelburg has hunted and captured every type of beast imaginable to man. Save one." He smiled. "And so we contracted Herr Shottelburg and his crew to come here, and once and for all, rid our land of this ferocious and homicidal demon."

A few in the audience clapped, and Shottelburg bowed in gratitude. Ruby's gloved hand tightened on Arthur's, and Stephen Compton continued. "As Herr Shottelburg is not a boastful man, I shall continue with our fearsome account. I, myself, joined Shottelburg's experienced troop and the eight of us journeyed into the darkest and most primitive parts of the Pine Barrens, the notorious haunt and home of the Leeds Devil. For weeks we searched, finding only peculiar hoof marks and tracks that vanished suddenly as if a horse had magically taken to flight. We found the remains of livestock, deer and dog. I apologize again, but their gruesome remains had been torn to shreds, ripped by long nail or fang, the bones flung in every direction. But, as we marched through the rank bogs, and hunted across the dark primordial pines, there was still no sign of the actual creature. At last, Herr Shottelburg conjured an idea. A thought so ghastly that I fear almost to speak it aloud here before women, before civilized men. But, to survive the darkest shores of Africa and endure the great mountains of the Orient and the ferocious beasts that dwell in those lands, one learns to no longer think as a civilized man. His suggestion was to set a trap. To bait the demon out with the promise of a meal. And,

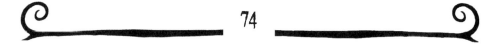

the bait, my dear civilized friends, was to be that of a five-year-old boy."

"Heavens," Ruby gasped, her hand now squeezing tightly. The reaction from the rest of crowd was a lingering rush of similar phrases and genuine shock. Arthur grinned eagerly.

"And not just any boy," their host added. "The sacrificial child would be Herr Shottelburg's very own son." More gasps. The hunter nodded solemnly. "A sometime traveling companion of his illustrious father, perhaps you have seen him scurrying about this very tent. While the rest of us stared in horror, and I implored the fierce hunter to find another way, it was the boy who interrupted the argument and set us on our final terrifying course. He, himself, agreed to the responsibility and said that he would, and I quote, 'Blissfully perform this perilous duty for my father, for the people of New Jersey and for God himself.'

Scattered applause.

"The boy was set in a small bog and told to sob loudly and occasionally cry out for help. Our party hid in the darkness of the trees just outside of view. At our call were several rifles and pistols, special nets and cages and enough rope to ensnare half the cattle in Texas. With the poor boy's cries spilling across the ominous pines, it wasn't long before *it* heard him. Then, it came for the boy. It came for its supper."

One audience member groaned loudly in revulsion and several men laughed. Ruby shook her head and Arthur carefully and quickly patted her leg in support. "It's just horrible," she whispered, eyes drawn sharply.

"I know, I know," Arthur said. "But remember, dear Ruby, that a bold heart is half the battle. And so, with two hearts, we shall be brave together." He smiled, and her eyes smiled back at him, as she squeezed his hand twice again tightly. Surely, the finest twenty cents in the history of man, Arthur thought proudly. Shottelberg and his son should be canonized.

"I shall not describe the thing to you now. For soon enough, you shall see the demon with your very eyes. Secondly, words can not justify the terror of it, the repulsiveness that we were to soon look upon that wicked day. It was exposed to us in the full view of daylight, this creature from nightmares. Several of Shottelberg's men, I regret to report, plainly went mad just to look upon it. They are, as we speak, still under a doctor's care. We have dimmed the lights here tonight in hopes that that shall not happen again. This is not a thing of nature, ladies and gentlemen, nor of our dear God. Shakespeare once asked, 'What Immortal Hand or Eye could make such a wretched beast?' and I thought of those words when the demon swooped into the bog on wings to devour the child."

While the crowd quietly conferred over that detail, Compton grabbed several items at his feet and then moved across the stage towards a young man in the front row. "You, sir," he said. "It would not surprise me if you were the strongest man in all the Garden State." The room chuckled as the man flexed one arm playfully. "Do you think you could bend this steel rod in half?" Compton asked, struggling to bow the bar in his own hands. "It's three inches thick and made of the best Pittsburgh steel. Quite sturdy stuff."

The man smiled sheepishly, but stood. "Very good, go on then," Compton urged and stepped back as the man grinned again at the crowd and leaned over to examine the rod. Several words of encouragement sprinkled throughout the room. Taking the bar in both hands, he made a quick motion with his forearms and then tried again, and again, upper arms quivering. "Try your knee," Compton suggested, and then led the crowd in a round of applause as the man tried once more.

"I can't, sir," he finally admitted, out of breath.

Arthur quickly rolled his eyes. "Rather," he whispered. "I should like to have had a go at that bar." Ruby only shrugged in response.

"Thank you, sir," said Compton. "Now, if someone else would like to feel this rope. It's also three inches thick and wound so tight that it feels like steel. Take a look," he handed the rope to another man in the front row. "Now just rip that thread in half, sir." The man laughed and pulled at the end of the rope. He then inspected the rope more closely as the older woman sitting next to him grabbed an end for her own inspection. "Go right ahead, madam," Compton grinned. "Give it a thorough look."

"That's fine rope," she affirmed.

"We brought seven nets that day," Compton announced moving back to center stage with the rope and steel dowel in hand. "Each twenty feet across and made with this same unbreakable rope. The Devil tore through every one of them. Each time another net dropped, it used its claws and teeth to rip through. This unbendable steel was used in two cages we'd built especially for the creature." He held the rod up again. "Not only did the beast bend the bars of the cage, it broke them, smashing the metal into shards with its terrible strength.

"With all the tools of modern man failing us thus, it was with great uncertainty that we shouldered our rifles and prepared to cut the monster down. We had heard that bullets could not harm it, that cannonballs had actually passed clean through it. These seemed like children's stories only minutes before, but now that we had seen the monster and its power for ourselves; we knew the stories to be true. It tossed the last shreds of cage aside and charged us directly. I held my rifle just so, hoping against hope the weapon would have some effect on the demon." Compton mimicked shouldering a rifle. "It was then that Herr Shottelburg coolly said, if I may sir," he turned to the hunter who merely nodded again. "He proclaimed, 'Gentlemen, all the weapons of man can not arm fear. Put down your rifles.'"

The room openly gasped. "Crazy fool," someone said loudly.

"Indeed," Compton said, "I thought the very same, sir. But as I turned and saw the look in Herr Shottelburg's eyes, and then the look of his own men as the same spread from face to face, I knew that we had hired the right gentleman for the task. And I, too, lay down my weapon."

Ruby patted Arthur's thigh. "Isn't this exciting?" she asked. "Real adventure, real bravery, here in New Jersey. Can you imagine such a thing?"

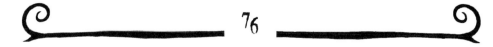

Arthur smiled thinly. He found the story rubbish, of course, but there was no denying that Ruby was enjoying it immensely. *But, was she scared enough?*

"I can't accurately describe what happened next," Compton told them. "I still awake most nights with the nightmares that remind me of what followed next. Thankfully, the images of night are fleeting. None of Herr Shottelburg's men, those who survived the ordeal, will discuss the matter further. In fact, most all of them have quit the business and have never been heard from again. By skill, luck, or the very grace of God, the creature was ultimately subdued. Muzzled. Chained. Caged again in even stronger steel. And at last brought here, tonight, to you."

The audience broke into excited side conversations as Compton stepped away from the stage and motioned to the curtain. "Ladies and gentlemen. The world-famous Davis Museum of Natural Wonders, in Philadelphia, is honored to present—The Leeds Devil."

The curtain pulled at once, and the entire room shifted suddenly to get a better look. The stage remained darker than the rest of the room, black shadows hovering over the steel cage and the still form laying within.

"Oh, Arthur," Ruby hissed next to him. "Is that . . . ? An actual monster." Her hand squeezed even tighter than before. The rest of the tent filled with hushed conversations and pointing.

Arthur remembered the news articles from a few years before and the descriptions of the Devil. He'd seen various artist renderings of the beast, some serious, most others down right comical in their playful portrayal of the various eyewitness accounts. But they did show the long horse face and legs, the strange eyes and tail, the dreadful bat wings. That same thing was now laying in the cage before him.

The fiend appeared massive, bulky weight trapped and compressed into a cage too small to reveal its true shape, the steel pen only three feet high so that the creature had to lay on its belly. They must do that to keep it under control, Arthur thought. Otherwise it might break free again. The body was covered in odd hair. Dirty, knotted, a strange color not of this world, as if it shimmered in hell fire.

One of the audience members rose from his chair to move around the first rows and get a closer look. "Please, sir," Compton warned. "Step not one foot closer. We dare not rile the beast." The man looked angrily at Compton and then considered the monster in the shadows before moving back to his chair.

The wings seemed not so much leathery as matted, as if they were peppered in ratty, grotesque, fur. But they were clearly large, a wingspan of at least ten feet from what Arthur could figure. The wings remained pressed closely against the beast's back. Probably clipped, he assumed optimistically.

It lay very still, but Arthur could still see its more subtle movements, the twitching snout, the faint lift of breath in its back. Its face was hidden partly in the darkness but, there too,

Arthur could make out some of the more dreadful features. It was indeed a horse's face. The extended sickening snout. A wet, fat nose. Arthur thought he could make out the row of razor-sharp teeth running along its mouth. It had bulbous eyes, eyes black as night, blacker even.

"The thirteenth child of a wicked woman, cursed from birth to become a monstrous demon."

Arthur shuddered. He found he'd moved ahead in his seat quite a bit, Ruby still clinging to his damp hand.

"I don't understand," Compton huffed suddenly.

Arthur looked quickly at Ruby and then back at their host. The room had grown absolutely quiet again.

"That . . ." Compton said. "That isn't his usual cage." He turned to Herr Shottelburg. "Find your men," he hissed.

At that precise moment, the beast struck, lurching from its motionless pose against the bars of the cage. The speed and ferocity with which the fiend moved gave the men no chance. The sound it made, the piercing demon bellow that rose from its throat filled the entire tent. The cage rattled loudly against the monster's assault, clanging against the stage, rattling violently. Most of the tent had jumped to its feet, Arthur and Ruby included.

"Arthur?" she gasped.

His eyes remained rooted on the cage. The Leeds Devil slammed once again against the thin metal bars.

And then the cage burst open.

Steel bars bounced and clattered in every direction, and the front of the cage fell away. The creature crawled free at last.

Chairs spilled in every direction as the room emptied through wide flaps now revealed at both sides of the tent. Ruby quickly found the closest door and turned back to grab hold of Arthur.

Arthur, who had fainted dead away just moments before, lay at her feet.

Ruby sighed deeply only once and then, jamming her purse sharply under her armpit, leaned into the still form of Arthur Pratt and lifted him onto her right shoulder. Slowly, she lurched with her load over several chairs and into the cool night air as cries from the carnival men throughout the park announced that the monster had already been recaptured.

They had dropped the tent flaps back into place when Compton turned to the rest of his team. "Okay, boys," he directed. "Another round in half an hour. Let's get the place cleaned up."

"You see that one guy pass out," the recent Herr Shottelburg asked. "Peaches. I mean, peaches!"

"You're a true fiend, Tommy Merril. I should put *you* in that cage some night. Help get

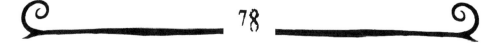

the chairs ready, would ya?"

"Sure, boss. Peaches."

Jack stepped from behind the curtain, a nine-year-old whose role was to poke the animal with a stick at just the right moment to get it riled up. At his side stood the beast. A five foot kangaroo purchased for eighty-nine dollars at a zoo in upstate New York. She'd been painted green, a light olive color that still came off on their hands every time they moved her. The wings on her back were made of wire and covered in a dozen different rabbit hides. Compton himself had crafted the belt that held on the clunky contraption.

"Hey, Jack," Compton called the boy closer. "You whacked our little Devil pretty hard tonight, didn't you?"

"No, sir," Jack replied, scratching fondly at the back of the kangaroo's head. "Same as always. Soon as you said 'find your men' I gave her a little nudge."

"Well, she sure took off tonight. Poor thing's just supposed to break the cage apart a bit and give 'em a bit of a scare while we direct them out. Not to break free and cause a genuine stampede."

"She's been pretty jumpy all night," the boy considered. "On edge, you know?"

"Okay, okay. Just take it easy this show, all right? We're moving on to Haddonfield tonight, and we don't need an upset mob of Quakers chasing after us, okay? Why don't you walk her back to the pen." He rustled the boy's hair. "You're doing fine, Jack. Just take it easy, okay?"

He watched the boy vanish through the back of the tent and then marched out front to check on the sales.

"Godamercy, Steve," the ticket master gawked. "What happened in there? That thing get out again?"

Compton smiled. "The cash, please. I counted twenty-two that round, right?"

"Yeah, Steve. Twenty-two. Gonna be pretty hard to get twenty more. Everyone's running around saying the Leeds Devil is free. Eating people and the like."

"Then we'll get thirty for sure," Compton winked and his ticket master held up his hands in surrender. "Wait a time more than usual, then start working the crowd again. Okay?"

"Sure thing, boss."

Compton grunted in response and stepped away. He inspected the cash bag quickly, enjoyed the weight of the coins within. Just about fifty dollars from Bridgeton by the end of the last show, he figured. Not bad, though not too good either considering the expenses of a five man team. But they'd be hitting other cities soon enough, bigger cities.

From behind their tent, he surveyed the crowd again. Decent size for a small town, with some spill-in from Burlington. He hoped word of the Devil's escape wouldn't reach too far from those who had already left the carnival. He should perhaps put out something in the paper about it, that there'd been a scare, but that the beast was certainly behind bars again.

Stretching his arms out wide, Compton shook out a day's worth of kinks and showmanship. It was then that he noticed the strange shape in the trees just outside of the carnival's lights. The silhouette of someone, something, watching. Watching him, he thought suddenly.

It was taller than a man. An odd hunched shape that half vanished into the trees beneath the dim glow of a crescent moon. He thought he saw something horse like in the shape, the long snout . . . .

"Blast," he cursed, angrily. "Jack!" he shouted out. "Jackie boy!"

"Yes, sir, Mr. Compton." The boy, huffing slightly, joined him behind the tents.

"Now, Jack," Compton intoned, putting his arm around the boy's shoulder. "I thought I told you to put that malodorous kangaroo in her pen."

"I did," the boy replied.

"Well, then she sure is in rare mood tonight," Compton snipped turning the boy towards the hulking black form in the woods. "Because she got out again."

The boy shook his head, pointing away from the dark tree line. "No, Mr. Compton, she's still there."

Compton frowned and slowly followed the path of the boy's finger to the tucked-away pen. Sure enough, a ridiculous green kangaroo stared back at him from inside its pen.

He took his hand off the boy's shoulder and turned again to the trees, expecting that the dark outline had vanished and that he could consider for years whether he'd ever seen the thing at all and whether or not it was . . .

But, that didn't happen. Because the dark thing hadn't moved an inch.

"Jack," he whispered. "Go get Tommy."

The boy vanished into the tent without another sound, and Stephen Compton was left alone with the thing in the woods. He sensed now, for sure, that it was watching him. He saw one of its globular red eyes glistening in the moonlight.

He took one step closer into the woods, and the thing moved. He recognized clearly that the head was horselike, the body looked heavier and taller than any man. He saw its wings now for the first time too.

Tommy Merril came running out of the tent with a lantern. "What is it, boss!" he shouted, "The kid said there's something weird out here."

At the bouncing light, the thing moved backwards into the night shadows of the trees. It had been more of of a hop, Compton thought. "Wait!" he half-shouted, half-gasped, his foot stepping forward over trembling leg. The wings spread out, and as quickly as Compton had taken his next step, the thing had bounced two more steps and then lifted on its wings back into the darkest night.

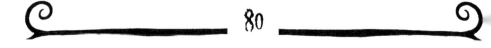

"What?" Tommy grunted. "What? What'd you see?"

"You didn't see that?" Compton snapped turning on him. "You're telling me you didn't see that?"

"See that? Yeah, I . . ." he stopped and shrugged, no longer looking at the trees. "No, boss. I didn't see nothin'."

Compton stared into the black woods. He wondered *if*, and he wondered *why*, and something of a shudder passed at last through his body. He shook it off and turned back to the tent. "I didn't see anything either," he said. "Thought I did."

Tommy nodded. "Yeah, these woods can get creepy. See some weird stuff, you know."

"Yeah."

"Saw a guy faint, though," Tommy laughed suddenly. "We sure saw that!"

"Yeah," Compton smiled weakly. "Yeah, we saw that." He scratched at the back of his head. "Tommy," he said. "Ask the boys to start tearing down, would you?"

"Tearing down? But we got a show.

"It's one show," Compton stopped him. "Everyone thinks the blasted thing is loose anyway. The whole carnival will be empty in fifteen minutes. I want to get on the road."

"So onto Haddonfield, yeah?"

"Yeah," Compton said. "I think it's best we get moving on. I'll bet there's some guy in Haddonfield's got ten cents—rather, twelve cents—for a chance to meet the very Devil himself."

NOTES: This story was based on a dozen different hoaxes and traveling sideshows that toured the East Coast from 1900 to 1960 purportedly showing the captured Leeds Devil or the creature's remains. A host of animals, carcasses, and sideshow theatrics were used to achieve the required demon. The most infamous show was that of Mr. Dave Jefferies of the 9th and Arch Museum in Philadelphia who, like others before and after, staged a capture, promoted the Devil, and then made a bundle off the lingering 1909 hype (the year the Jersey Devil achieved his most press). The green-painted kangaroo was very real—and thanks to Mr. Jefferies for the idea.

GHOSTS
1954

Repentance is a virtue only of fools and ghosts. Charlie Pynn grimaced as the old proverb ran through his head. "You don't say," he muttered. Looking at the house again for the first time in more than thirty years, he wasn't so sure.

The home was a decayed heap, rotted and forgotten. Between its sun-baked greyness and the water-soaked boards bending away at odd angles, it looked more like the remains of an excavated corpse than that of any home.

"So that's it, huh?" Pete Brickner stamped his cigarette and reached into his jacket for his pack.

Charlie unconsciously dragged his own boot across the butt. "Yeah," he said. "That's it."

"Looks like fifty other joints we've knocked down."

"Sure does." Charlie reached back inside the truck and killed the headlights.

"You'd think there'd be some news guy out here or something," Brickner continued, squinting into the breaking dawn. "Snapping some last photographs before it turns into a flat-land."

"There are a dozen towns from here to Voorhees that claim to have the exact same house. Even if the city boys knew the real one was here, they'd just get lost."

Brickner smiled. "Where's Voorhees?"

"Thirty minutes that way," Charlie pointed towards his boyhood home.

"Yeah? Your posse ever run up here?"

Charlie snorted. "Couple times, I guess."

Brickner laughed, looking at the house, then back at Charlie. "You're kidding! Oh, that's just great. That's . . . that's kismet. That's what this job is. It's kismet."

"Kismet," Charlie winced. "You been reading the funnies again?"

Brickner just laughed again, lighting his cigarette and blowing the smoke into the cold morning air. "You afraid of the boogie man, boss?"

"Always," Charlie smiled some. "Always."

"Can't believe you guys actually used to come up here."

"Kid stuff. Follow the tracks a bit, hike into the woods." He, too, now turned to the house. "Then we'd stare at an old house and dare each other to go inside."

Brickner's chuckle was warm, rich with his own memories, and he took another drag on

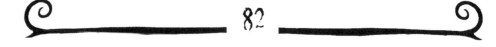

his cigarette. "I'll bet you did."

Charlie pointed to the split rail fence still running across the left-front corner of the property. "They used to say that he'd sit there at times, you know, watching his family. And that he still comes back sometimes. Still thinks of it as home."

"The Jersey Devil." Brickner shook his head. "Fantastic."

"Jersey Devil," Charlie said. "Leeds Devil, Mr. Leeds. Whatever. We called him lots of things. Great stories around a camp fire, you know."

"You ever seen anything up here?"

Charlie turned to him, managed a smile.

"You're killin' me, Pynn. You saw this thing?"

He shrugged. "Maybe" he said. "Saw something . . ." He watched the decrepit house. "One time, my brother David and his friends came up here and let me tag along."

"You never mentioned a brother, boss."

Charlie shrugged and said, "USS Monaghan, '44. Sank in a typhoon in the Pacific, never found him."

Brickner shook his head. "Yeah, yeah."

"But we always came up here." Charlie followed the memory, dragged along by the reminiscences of youth and the ancient house before him, silhouetted in early-morning sun. "Stared at the place for an hour or so, you know, kind of walking around it, tossing rocks through empty windows." He smiled. "Then the daring would start. Who'd step on the porch? Who'd touch the door? Who'd go inside and how far?"

"Anyone go inside?"

"Sometimes," Charlie nodded. "The real game was to scratch your name in whatever room you got to. 'R. Finckle, 1920,' you know? A permanent record, a bragging right, to mark who'd been where and when. Each new year, each town, pushing ever deeper into that horrible house."

"You go in?"

Charlie nodded. "Yeah, I've been in."

"Your name's in there?"

"No," Charlie replied. "Never did that. Meant to do it the last night I ever came up here but . . . just didn't."

Brickner grinned over his cigarette. "I think I like this story already, boss."

Charlie smiled back. "Yeah, okay. I was ten, and my brother and the other guys were twelve, thirteen, I guess. We all went up together and stood on the porch. Four of us. Figured we could get pretty far into the house if we all stuck together. It was cooler to do it yourself, of course, but we figured if we got our four names scratched in that back bedroom or, man-oh-man, on the basement door, we'd remain legends forever. Most kids never made it past the front door."

"It's just a house," Brickner said.

"Maybe," Charlie replied. "Yeah, sure it is. But you didn't grow up with the same stories we did. Demon births and monsters in the cellar, the bones of the Leeds family all over the yard. My grandmother used to tell us that Mother Leeds still lived in the house. That she was using some of her witching powers to stay alive all those long years, waiting for her youngest son to return."

"Your grandmother told you this?"

"No kidding," Charlie laughed. "Now toss in the ghosts of the entire murdered Leeds family. *And* these other ghosts that were supposed to haunt the place—friends of Mr. Leeds, they told us."

Brickner laughed again. "Hello, Mary! You Pineys sure come up with some stories out here, don't you? No wonder most of you never made it past the front door."

Charlie nodded. "We sure made it past that day. Stepped right into the main room, brave as King Arthur's knights."

"How far'd you all get?"

"You gonna let me tell the story?"

"Please," Brickner held out his hand in apology.

"I'd stood in the doorway the time before, but had never actually gone in before. This time, we all took a walk in the front room. There was a bunch of garbage. Bottles and rocks that half a century of kids had thrown into the place, and it looked like any furniture had been lifted by souvenir hunters. And sure enough, there were the names scratched into the walls and floor. I think I'd counted twenty when David called us. Said he knew where the back bedroom was."

"Where it was born?"

"So they say. The room was filthy, dusty. Again, everything worth anything had already been lifted. You could still see on the floor where there'd been a bed. There were . . . We thought maybe we'd found old blood stains on the floor, too. And, there were strange mark-ings on the walls, strange drawings that someone had scratched in many years before. And I'll tell you, I wouldn't want to meet the person who done those drawings."

"Guess not."

"I counted seven names in the whole room. Seven kids in fifty years that had even made it that far. Jimmy and Ray started carving their names into the floor right away beside where the bed must have been. I pulled out my own pocket knife and started thinking about where to make my mark. Couldn't take my eyes off those other carvings, though. Or, the strange stains on the wood floor. Then, David told us he wanted to go all the way."

"What'd that mean?"

"The cellar. Yeah boy, Davie wanted us to go all the way to the cellar where she'd kept the monster locked up all those years. Jimmy and Ray said they were up for it until they realized he was serious. But big brother hadn't even taken out his knife yet. He said he was gonna wait. We stumbled on his heels through the kitchen where we found stairs that led upstairs and the door."

"Door to the cellar."

"Yeah. There were two of them actually. The first was opened just a crack, and David worked up the nerve to pry it open all the way. I can tell you my heart was thumpin' like it never has since. Jimmy wouldn't even look when he did it. I don't know what we expected to see. Maybe Mother Leeds herself would come running out, a frazzle-haired witch with nails like knives. Maybe the Devil himself. Maybe nothing but darkness. Darkness that hid things even more horrifying than witches and demons."

Brickner nodded, not speaking, and Charlie continued. "But when that big door swung open, and sunlight spilled inside for the first time in who knows how long, all we saw was another door. I could tell the others were relieved. But not David. I saw nothing but disappointment in his face. There was one name on that second door." He thought for a moment. "It read, 'Waldin, 1918,' and there was cold air coming from under the bottom of the door. Jimmy and Ray had it. Didn't even want to put their names on the door. What followed next I can only guess at now. It was the unique argument that boys have and was spoken in language and stances a man can't translate." Plus," he winked, "I was absolutely terrified by that point."

Charlie started walking slowly towards the house. Brickner followed closely behind, and they stopped at the front steps.

"The next thing I knew," Charlie said, "Jimmy and Ray were heading upstairs, my brother was fiddling with that cursed basement door, and I was standing back in the front room again all by myself. By now, of course, it's getting darker and late afternoon shadows are turning into early evening shadows. I danced between the front room and doorway, rooting for the sun to stay up. Willing it above these blasted trees." He ran his finger across the sky, tracing the tall pines surrounding the lot, even now filtering the sun's early light. "I kept yelling for them to hurry up. Every so often I'd hear them yelling back at me to 'shut up,' and I'd hear the boards creak above me. And I heard other things too, I suppose."

"Other things?"

"I don't know. Maybe just the wind pushing through busted shutters. But something. Something lighter, icier than the regular creeks and groans of an old house. It kind of moved through the house like an old, soft tune. Something I could almost hear if I tried hard enough. *Almost* . . . . Then they started screaming."

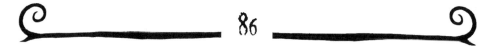

"Screaming?" Brickner yelped the word.

"Jimmy, or Ray. I'm not sure which one I heard first. But it was both of them, soon enough, and they were coming down those steps again like a herd of buffalo. I'm amazed they didn't just bust straight through the ceiling. They came spinning into the living room looking like mad men. Eyes wide as white-walled tires."

"What'd they see?" Brickner threw down his cigarette and stamped it dead, his eyes riveted on Charlie. "What happened up there?"

"Ray just ran right past me. I think Jimmy might have stopped some to drag me along with him. I yelled at them about David, told them we had to get David. But, Ray was already halfway down the road, and Jimmy wasn't budging a hair. We yelled for David from the doorway, but didn't hear anything back. Jimmy wouldn't tell me what they saw. He kept telling me to be quiet. Kept cursing our own stupidity. I begged him to go back in with me to find David, but he said he couldn't. Not that he wouldn't, but that he couldn't."

"You went in."

"Yeah, I went in. I never got passed the kitchen though. Stood up top, looking through those two cellar doors. Guess he'd gotten the second door open after all. I started wondering why someone would put two doors over the same room and wobbled some at the answer. I called out for him. Screamed his name a dozen times, but nothing. Then, I heard the steps leading upstairs. A creak, a footstep maybe, and I dashed around the corner hoping it was David. It wasn't."

"What'd you see, Charlie?"

"I don't know. Nothing. Maybe I didn't see anything. I was ten, I was terrified. Shadows playing funny off the walls. Jimmy and Ray had kicked up a lot of dust maybe. But . . ."

"What'd you do?"

"I ran." Charlie said simply. "Faster than I ever have in my life. Where David was, at that moment, or what . . . what fate I'd left him to, I didn't know. I just ran." He tried to smile, but from the look on his colleague's face, he knew he wasn't doing a very good job of it.

Brickner nodded, uncomfortably. Charlie Pynn's eyes and thoughts were somewhere else. "Then he came out?" he asked, his voice encouraging.

"David? Sure," Charlie said softly. "Sure, he did. Me and Jimmy were standing out on the front steps, Ray still waiting for us down the road. Both of us panting like dogs out of breath, and shaking from head to toe. And the next you know, Davie just comes walking out the front door."

Brickner laughed. "No!"

"Yeah," Charlie grinned, pointing. "He just walks down those steps like he'd just left a movie."

"How far?"

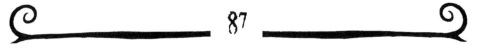

"Into the house?" Charlie looked at Brickner. "Told us he walked all around the cellar."

Brickner snorted laughter. "The cellar! That's gotta be the all-time record."

"Maybe, maybe."

"You believe him?" He asked, whimsically.

Charlie thought for a moment. "I like to," he said. "I like to."

"It's a shame about your brother, Charlie. Bet he'd have gotten a kick out of us out here today."

"Yeah," Charlie nodded, his smile tight. "He would have."

"Kids," Brickner laughed. "Nothing changes."

"I suppose," Charlie replied, shaking away a previous thought. "Some kid broke both his legs messing around out here just a few months ago. State police used to chase us away too."

"So now we knock it down."

"Kismet, right? Guess it's time to unload the bulldozer."

"I got it, boss," Brickner said. "Why don't you take a look around the place again. Any sink holes or wells? Make sure there no kids hiding in there."

Charlie looked at Brickner and knew his colleague was intentionally offering him space. Trouble was, he needed it. "Okay," he said.

He took a quick walk about the yard, surprised at how little things had changed. The few times they'd come up as kids, they'd spent the bulk of the day wandering about the yard. Playing around the fence. *The same fence the Leeds Devil had played around.* He remembered perfectly where the well was, and made a mental note to fill it. He came upon the old pump and the rows of flowers—gentian, frostweed, and birdfoot violets, and also rocks, that were surely once put over the graves of the four generations of Leeds. Then, he went into the house again.

The front room was also the same as he had remembered. More garbage certainly. Soda and beer bottles. He could see where someone had started a fire in the corner of the house. Vandalism, perhaps. Perhaps something else. Dust and silvery cobwebs shimmered in the fresh sunlight coming through the opened door and windows. The black hole of the large fireplace gaped at him from across the room.

The boards creaked under Charlie's feet with each slow step, echoing through the house. In the back bedroom, the shutters were gone, the sun flooding the room in strange pockets of warm light while other spots remained in total shadow. He stepped in confidently to look around.

Charlie Pynn did not know much about mental illness. He wasn't a doctor of psychiatry. But even at ten he had recognized the scrawlings, the illustrations, of total madness. Now, they seemed even more insane, more horrible.

Some were carved by blade, some clearly scratched as if done by nails. There were pictures stained, painted with some dark substance, and other symbols burned into the walls and floor. They covered the room. A single dire eye drawn over and over again. Shapes and characters repeated across the one wall, symbols and runes running over childlike images of a family, of some macabre bat thing. Other images, too, but Charlie would not look at them. He could not wrap his head around what they meant, what they hinted at. They were of things more horrible than deformed sons and winged beasts. These other images, Charlie thought, were not something that were ever meant to be drawn by man. How the Leeds family came to them, or who had recorded them would never be known. Charlie was glad of that.

He turned away from the ghoulish images, focusing instead on the names on the floor, the names honored in the wood. He found the carvings left by Jimmy and Ray easily. Laughed quietly at the memory and his discovery, and he hoped the chuckle would help chase away the chill that was already creeping up his back. A chill that carried the notion that he should never have come back into the house, that someone, or something, was in the house with him even now. And, that he had seen that same something thirty years before.

He found that he'd moved into the kitchen, though he hadn't remembered walking there. The first door to the basement hung only by its top hinge, but it was still shut, the door behind it lost in shadowed darkness. Beyond the kitchen was the bottom of the steps that led upstairs. He marveled again at how familiar the place remained. A place he'd only stood in once, thirty years before. The steps' hallway was darkened, the sunlight barely reaching into the kitchen. He switched on his flashlight and pointed it up the wooden stairs. Cobwebs filled the exposed beams running alongside and above the steps. He stomped his foot on the first step, and it groaned under the test. He took the next few steps the same, slowly, his flashlight dancing nervously about the passage. He thought now about what he'd seen on these same steps thirty years before. Or what, perhaps, he only thought he'd seen.

The man he'd seen in the hallway that dark day, flickering faintly in the shadowed dust-filled passage, had been dressed in a short coat with broad, plate buttons and pants shredded and fluttering at the bottoms. He had no shoes or stockings but wore a sling over his shoulders which carried three pistols. Around his waist, a sash which carried a dagger at least a foot long. A pirate, Charlie had thought, shocked at the notion. Then, he forgot that point in favor of another realization. The man had no head.

Mouth hanging open in astonishment, eyes squinting up the dim stairway, Charlie at ten had been sure of it. The coat, the dark shape, simply stopped at the neck. Grisly strands of skin and bone hinted at the loose collar.

He knew the tales of the notorious Captain Kid and the treasures he and his bandit crew had buried up at Barnegat Bay. And he'd heard of the shipmate who'd been beheaded so that his ghost would forever guard the Captain's treasure. Charlie'd also heard that the same lonely ghost had eventually met and befriended a fiend along the sandy marshes of the Atlantic. *A fiend called Leeds.*

He'd frozen up stiff then. Despite his desire to run, it was as if a spell had been placed upon him, a curse meant to keep him within reach. The man at the top of the stairs—the shimmering apparition, the *thing*—then flowed unhurriedly down the steps towards him. His gnarled hand had dropped to the sash to draw the sinister blade free. Charlie's hand had clung to the side of the stairwell for support.

It was then that he saw the second ghost. Another figure who'd appeared as if through the wall itself, a shower of golden light emerging through wood beams. Standing between the boy and the headless spirit.

Charlie shook off the memory, stepping across the same steps he'd seen the . . . seen *something*. The remaining boards creaked loudly with each slow step. At the top of the landing, he looked down again into the dark stairway and appraised his climb, breathing heavily.

On the second floor, several holes in the roof allowed the sun's first rays to filter into the room in beautiful shards of light. He wondered now if that is all he had seen that day. Light playing through a broken roof, shadows playing through a broken house.

The figure, the woman, had been beautiful. At ten, he'd read enough fairy tale books to know a beautiful girl when he saw one. Her hair was golden and flowed about her face as if it were an energy unto itself, carried in eternal ghostly wind. Her gleaming robe fluttered gracefully about her slender shape, her arms lifting as if starting a waltz. The face was indeed that of a princess, though bright in a shining light that soon filled the stairway in its brilliance. Cold air had flowed down the steps, blowing Charlie's hair back from his face just before he managed to flee the house.

Now, Charlie quickly viewed the upstairs, peeking briefly into each of the rooms. Many of the quarters remained lost in shadows so deep that even his flashlight could not cut through the grimy darkness. He leaned closer into the darkened rooms, the boards under his boots rotten and unsafe. He heard the bulldozer's engine start up and stepped back to peek out an upper window. He watched Brickner begin to back the bulldozer onto the ground.

He turned to the dark rooms a final time, once more casting his light into the unyielding darkness. He breathed in cold morning air, dirty with age, and then moved towards the stairway again. Charlie took the steps slowly, walking sideways so that his back never completely faced the second floor.

In the kitchen the double doors to the cellar waited.

Charlie studied them briefly, grabbed the inside of the first busted door and slowly pulled it back and to the side. Another hard yank and the top hinge burst free from the decayed wood. The door came free in his hand and he set it against the wall. The second door, he noticed, now for the first time, had been painted red. A dark crimson that ignored the morning sunlight. Four names had been carved on the door. Charlie recognized none of them. The last name had been carved in '48.

There were two rusted deadbolts crossing both the top and bottom of the second door.

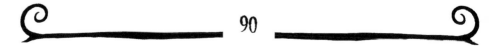

Neither was closed. From rusty marks and blots, Charlie could see where nails and other boards had once been used to seal the second door. Once long ago, he thought, and took hold of the door's handle.

The door opened easily, as if it had wanted to be opened and had merely been waiting for the excuse. Total darkness seeped from the room within and crept around the door frame into the kitchen. Charlie pulled the door ajar completely and hoped the sunlight would make a sporting go of it. The sunlight made it only so far as the second step. Beyond that, only Charlie's flashlight could go. The beam cut again into the blackness, and some shape of the cellar began to form.

Narrow stone steps led into the dank cellar. He could make out the left wall and figured the room was maybe only six feet high. The smell was stale and wet as Charlie took the first step into the room. Ice ran up his legs and back. Another step and more of the room filled in the electric torch's light.

The room was completely empty. The floor was covered in water-rotted boards, the walls in uneven rows of damp wide stone. Scattered about the floor Charlie's light revealed tattered clothing or a blanket. He saw a broken jug or two, and found bones of various sizes dotted about the room.

He looked up suddenly, half expecting that the second door had just been slammed shut. That he was trapped forever in the same dark tomb that the Leeds' youngest child had once been locked in two hundred years before.

Instead, when he looked up, he saw the scratching on the walls. His flashlight's beam moved across the marks slowly. They were not made by human hands, and they were not made by some blade. He knew now for certain that something with claws had once been trapped in this same cellar, something large and powerful, something with claws, five to each hand, that had scratched briefly at the wall. Something patiently looking for a way out.

He looked away from the hideous markings and cast his eyes to the floor again, hoping to chase away the new images in his mind. It was then that he saw it.

Carved into the floor, washed out some in the mold-spotted wood. Dark and faded.

David '24'

Charlie kneeled down to the carving and ran his fingers across the letters. "David," he said aloud into the darkness. "You son of a gun. You really did." He laughed suddenly, uncaring of the house he'd entered, the infamous dwelling he'd just explored. "I always knew it," he said, smiling. He fondly tapped the faded characters again. "I shouldn't have run, David," he said into the darkness. "I . . . ."

He stopped himself and coughed out the sudden knot in his throat. The black walls of the cellar throbbed around him, alive somehow in their damp chill. Alive in their memories of things best forgotten. And yet, the chill that he'd been carrying for the past fifteen minutes, or perhaps longer he thought, lifted.

He pulled the knife from his back pocket and slowly started carving.

NOTES: Many homes are believed to be that of the Jersey Devil. Leeds Point and Burlington are the two most popular sites, and state police have been chasing the curious away from such homes for almost two hundred years. The Shrouds House, found on Leeds Point, may be the most popular. Its picture is featured in *The Jersey Devil* and subsequently, a hundred internet sites. That house was demolished in 1954. The headless pirate and golden girl stories are also part of the Jersey Devil myth.

INTO THE ABYSS
1969

The razor-sharp proboscis ripped into Joe Castner's skin, and a dripping jagged spike emerged from the gruesome creature's snout, sinking even deeper into the torn flesh. The pain was immediate and fiery. Its saliva spewed over the fresh wound and mixed instantly with Joe's own blood like some alien virus, preventing coagulation to make him bleed even more. The monster dipped its head lower still and began to feast, filling its already gorged belly with Joe's blood.

"Thanks so much," Joe grimaced.

The mosquito lifted from his arm in response and vanished again into the night. Joe ticked off another number on his sheet and kept his arm up for other potential munchers. The quick field test was all part of a report he'd turn in at the end of the week and, surprisingly, one of the more pleasant assignments he'd received to date working for the New Jersey Mosquito Control Commission. He glanced again at his watch. "Two minutes," he said and brought his arm back down. "Six landings. Not bad at all."

He tossed just half a scoop of the granular abate chemical into the small pond, then moved back towards his jeep. The dark green automatic had proved perfect for getting around the bogs and sand dunes of the New Jersey Pine Barrens, just like the jeeps he'd driven overseas. He climbed inside and grabbed the map again. "Just one more," he spoke to himself, pushing back his glasses. "Then this little piggie is going home."

He looked out into the dark pines, and a cold shudder briefly raced across his back. Overtime on the night shift was fine pay for a graduate student attending Rutgers University, but he could probably do without the scary Pine's business. The other guys had teased him plenty about various ghosts, and witch houses, and some devil creature. They'd even warned him of magical blue ponds in the woods that were said to lead straight to Hell. *Quite a place to earn a buck.*

Joe started the truck, and the engine's rumble immediately filled the dark forest. He pulled away from the small marsh and moved eastward deeper into the pines, glancing out the side and marking the moon's location. Even though, or maybe because, he'd been with the Mosquito Commission four months, and had survived a tour in the jungles of Vietnam, he knew it was still very easy to get lost in the endless pines. Just two weeks before, they'd had to send in some state foresters to find Hank Wasson, a ten-year pro who'd gotten turned around and lost pretty good working along the Nescochague Creek. And that was in broad daylight!

He snaked down something called Hollow Road, and the squat truck's headlights cut a narrow path through the darkness as its wheels crunched over gloomy underbrush. He passed several narrow pathways leading away from the main trail and counted each. "Inskips Creek should be right here," he muttered, shifting into first and slowing the truck. He reached out the window and grabbed hold of the small spotlight attached there. Pointing it forward into the dark trees, he flipped it on.

Something screeched at him. An animal of some kind shrieked in a piercing and dreadful yelp of complaint, the sound of an animal in pain. Frowning, Joe pulled the truck forward and swiveled the light deeper into the woods.

He saw movement, some dark shape scampering through the trees away from him. A deer, perhaps. He stopped the truck and reached into the tool box for the large flashlight before climbing slowly out of the truck. The headlights cast wraithlike shadows of mist on the trail just ahead, but the spotlight on the side of the truck seared through the trees. He aimed it towards the creek and started towards where he thought the creek should be. The air smelled odd as he moved further into the trees, thick and sulfuric.

Behind him, something large moved quickly in the woods, crushing underbrush with each step. But, the hint of danger didn't occur to him. Instead, Joe's ears picked up on the strange gurgling sound he heard, a faint pop and bubble that sounded just like a fresh bowl of Rice Krispies.

His flashlight fell upon the creek, the small natural waterway he'd been assigned to test for mosquito larva and treat if necessary. Then, he saw it.

A single dead fish floated just within the beam of his light. The pickerel's saucer-like black eye and silver scales gleamed in the unnatural light as the dark water popped in endless bubbles around the fish. Spitting and fizzing, the water boiled over the very sides of the creek. Joe Castner fell back a step.

The creek was boiling!

Not frothing in pollution or detergents, nor foaming in algae or disease. And, it wasn't filled with emerging and gyrating tadpoles and mosquitoes larvae. The water was literally boiling over, like a pot left too long on the stove.

"That's . . ." Joe moved the flashlight along the creek and the beam skipped in his trembling hand as he found more fish floating dead in the bubbling water. "That's impossible." Curious, he took another step towards the creek. He thought briefly of going back to the truck to get gloves and tubes to take an actual water sample.

The brief thought distracted him, and in a sudden moment of clarity, he heard the sound again, the crunching sound of something heavy moving through the woods. Joe swallowed. It moved more slowly now, however, deliberate, like a man would. Not some wild beast scurrying through the woods to get to its home before dark. But something else.

Joe stood frozen for one long moment more. Then, he sprinted toward the truck. His steps were frenzied, his legs moving faster than his own feet could go, and full branches smacked at his face and hands as he navigated an uneven course, sweeping past whatever tree would get him to the truck's lights the soonest.

He cursed as he leaped into the driver's seat, where he fell over the steering wheel, panting heavily to catch his breath. When he finally did, he started to chuckle. "What a dope," he moaned. A scared dope.

A powerful jolt from behind snapped Joe's head forward, and he crashed against the wheel. Something had smashed into the jeep. Another car? He grunted in surprise and twisted to see what had hit him, his glasses hanging half off his face.

Over the small barrels of chemicals and equipment, and through the back flap, he first saw only night and the jagged blackness of the trees which framed the path he'd just come down. He set straight his glasses and looked again. Something else moved in the darkness just behind the jeep. A large unnatural shape, some animal moving just behind him and coming up along the back of the vehicle. A plump, rounded back. Like a bear, maybe, he thought, casting about to classify the creature. Then, red eyes glared in the back isinglass window.

Joe Castner started the jeep and floored the gas in the same motion.

The jeep's engine roared in response, and the tires dug in deep as he pushed it to thirty and raced down the sandy trail. He figured the animal now stood a hundred yards behind him. Shocked and still choking on sand dust, Joe shifted into third, and the trees and darkness fell away before the headlights in a rush of bullying black shadows.

He squinted over the hood, leaning above the wheel and following the murky trail in fleeting images. He knew he was going too fast. It was too dark, and a sharp curve or a fallen tree would prove disastrous at best. Easing off the gas, he brought the jeep down to only fifteen miles per hour.

Joe screamed. It was more like the shriek of a little girl, he admitted immediately, but his fingers gripped the wheel all the same. He'd caught just a glimpse of "it" moving in the corner of his eye. The thing, some *creature*, just beside his jeep. Setting his jaw as he pressed his boot more deliberately on the gas pedal, he risked another look.

The thing was large, its dark outline almost even with the open side of the vehicle, and it moved on all fours. It loped, running beside him like a gorilla, just beside his seat. Another one, he told himself. There must be a pack of them!

His boot stomped on the gas again, and he turned into the animal hoping to scare it off, or force it back into the woods. Instead, the creature slammed against the side of the jeep and the jar of the collision rocked Joe in his seat. He cursed again, half frustrated he'd hit the animal. He hoped he hadn't hurt it too badly and that it would simply scamper off again in the darkness with its friends. Joe turned his full attention back to the narrow dirt road.

He felt a weight drop onto the jeep's canvas roof then, the impact thunderous and abrupt. The vehicle lurched sideways against the force, and Joe yanked on the wheel against the skid. Something ripped through the top, shredding away at the canvas with its claws.

In the mirrors he saw a dark hulking shape clinging now to the backside of the jeep. It pulled itself higher onto the roof, claws scraping and clicking, looking for a way inside. Looking for him!

Nothing but trees ahead, as the road split right and left, and Joe shifted into first again, gunning into a hard right turn to shake the creature off. The cans and barrels rattled in the cabin behind him, tumbling over each other. The jeep jerked sideways, swerving so badly he thought it might tip. He held his breath waiting for the impending crash into the black trees.

Instead, the tires spun wide, sliding against the sand, and he gassed it again, fighting for control of the vehicle as it careened down the trail. The path grew narrower, the trees stretching overhead like a black canopy. The jeep's tires bounced over dense underbrush, jerking back and forth as he settled into control again. He looked back.

Nothing.

Adrenalin flooded through him so forcefully his head swam, and Joe turned back again just in time to realize the jeep was spinning toward a thick stand of pines.

Feet from impact, Joe swerved into the only possible opening. The next instant, the dirt road became an overgrown trail, the beam from his headlights ricocheting madly off of thick black trunks. The back of the jeep slammed against one of the trees, and Joe stamped on the brakes, flopping over the rough terrain for several more feet, and then crashed to a sudden stop.

The headlights pointed downward; the light reflected in an orange glow surrounding the front of the jeep. He'd driven into a ditch, the two front tires had fallen into the deep sandy rut. "Swell," he muttered. He sighed deeply and leaned back against the seat with his eyes closed.

Then, a deep chill worked its way down his spine. Joe reached over slowly for the flashlight, which had fallen to the floor. His perception and tolerance of fear had certainly altered a great deal while overseas. There was no denying what a long night in the Central Highlands of Vietnam could do for a young man's view of such things—but he still recognized fear's probing and icy prickle well enough. I'm in danger, his instincts hissed. There's something bad out here, and I'm sure as heck not going to sit in this jeep and wait for it to find me. His hand found the flashlight, and he pulled himself up straight again. His other hand grabbed the wheel for balance and, taking a resolute breath, he stepped out into the Pine Barrens.

The supernatural glow of the half-buried headlights washed over his boots and legs and he stumbled away from the jeep, his legs still quivering from the sudden stop. The ground was uneven and covered in prickly thick underbrush. Thorns stabbed into his legs, poking at him from the darkness and pulling at his pant leg.

Joe kicked off the briars and turned back towards the jeep, running his flashlight over the front. The trench was natural and shallow enough that'd he'd be able to wedge the jeep out again, and he flashed the light around looking for a suitable log.

Noise crunched in the dark woods behind the jeep. The now familiar crackling of leaves and sticks under heavy steps. He thought of the shovel, the one in the back of the jeep. A perfect weapon if . . . .

Joe glanced up, then staggered away from the dim flush of the headlights.

The creature stood full atop the jeep.

He remembered the first time he'd seen a water buffalo at night, when the enormous shape and broad horned head rose over the black lines of swaying East-Asian grass like some wicked primordial god. For a kid from the streets of Cleveland, it had proven quite a sight. He'd not yet shaken the creepy image from his many grim memories. He smiled weakly, thinking of it now. The creature on the jeep looked much worse.

A sinister and brooding hulk rose up over the truck, cast in headlight-fumed shadows and night. It even had the same face as the buffalo, the long snout and sharp ears silhouetted in sharp lines against the forest's darkness. Joe's arm dropped limply to his side, his flashlight not forgotten. He saw where the creature's legs had stretched out over the length of the top of the truck. The monster crept forward slowly, its snout pressed low to the roof. Its sniffing sounds were grisly, filling the woods with short coarse snorts. The claws of its front legs scratched callously against the vehicle's canvas top, tearing away more of the fabric. The heavy thump of its hind legs scuffing the jeep proved even louder as the black profile of a long tail coiled out behind the shadowy beast.

The eyes were crimson spheres smoldering like tiny fires. As if hearing his thoughts, they turned slowly towards him. Immense wings spread behind the same cruel eyes, and Joe's vision tunneled until all he saw were the wide black flaps and the glowing eyes.

Joe backed deeper into the woods, his eyes full on the creature. It crawled slowly like some great spider down the front of the jeep onto the hood. The man-sized monster crouched over the headlight's glow as if warming itself by a fire and its long hairy neck stretched deeper into the glow, shadows casting over its face.

Joe ran. Dashing into the woods, he flipped the flashlight off and weaved though the trees only by moonlight. The May brush remained thick and grasping, but he pushed through with the genuine determination of fear. Over the roar of his own pounding boots he could hear the creature behind him. And it was following.

Joe stumbled through the trees for what seemed like far too long, staggering between glimpses of trees and mist. His ragged breath and the next flash of trees became his only focus. Time became broken, meaningless, as he tried to wake from the nightmare that he knew in his heart wasn't a nightmare at all. He was caught in that hideous halfway point between the waking world and a dream with lousy reception. And, always, it followed, too close behind.

He fell forward and collapsed against a thick red maple, listening for the beast, trying to pick out its sounds in the gloom.

He struggled to pull together his recon of the creature. It was big. It moved fast. Joe

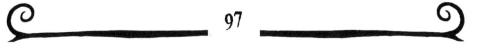

guessed the thing was seven feet long and almost two hundred pounds. It was definitely an animal of some kind running across the carpet of sand and shrubs on two legs. Two legs!

Joe broke into a second half-blind sprint through the murk and stumbled again across the shrub-littered ground. The creature pursued him still, and Joe found strength in his legs to run even faster. While he ran, a gruesome howl roared after him, forcing him to hold his hands to his ears.

A flash of light caught his eye from the right and Joe turned towards it. The forest opened up just ahead and he ran for the light as best he could. Maybe it was a road or a hunting cabin or . . . .

He staggered into the clearing, stepping over the last line of thorns and ivy, and stood on the shore of a dark lake. The moon's light reflected off the still black water, mirrored as a lone light in the pond's darkness. Behind him the creature screamed, swaying, swooping, stomping through the tangled underbrush. Getting closer.

It was going to kill him, he realized suddenly. The thought unnerved him, rendered him helpless. It seemed too random and without point. Before, he'd faced violence and danger that had a name, that had some historical and realistic context of chance and reason that he eventually learned to wrap his head around. But, this? This thing was something else.

He looked around the lake. It was too dark to see anything beyond the surrounding treeline. Miles of desolate forest in every direction. *And, this creature owned the forest.* That much was certain. He couldn't hide from the thing in the woods, couldn't outrun it. The forest was no longer an option.

He stole a final glance back at the sounds in the trees coming towards him, then crashed toward the safety of the dark waters. Joe stumbled awkwardly into the lake, the cold water running up his pants, boots sinking into the sandy bottom. He felt numb from the first step. Icy. The water went up past his waist now and, moving ever deeper into the lake, he turned back to find the creature.

Its black shape stood along the shoreline watching him, ember-red eyes fixed on Joe's own. It sat low, crouched over its fat hind legs as Joe continued deeper into the water. It had stopped.

The cold water rose higher, heavy against his chest now. The creature leaned forward and lapped at the water's edge, and the wings lifted over its head again, bizarre blade-like shapes that hung over its misshapen form. The next step brought water to Joe's chin, and he stopped. Far enough. He looked about the small pond for the quickest way out and seemed to be close to its dead center.

The creature barked suddenly, a shrill yelp that echoed over the lake. Three times, the ghastly call went out. The sound of warning, Joe thought. Or the sound of frustration at an escaped meal. But, as the thing backed away into the woods, it occurred to Joe that it also sounded like something else. For a moment, it sounded almost as if the beast were simply

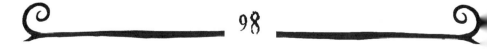

laughing at him.

The chuckling shape vanished again behind the treeline.

He waited for several minutes, or seconds or hours; he wasn't exactly sure. One thing he'd learned in the army, was that time had a funny way of warping depending on what was going on around you. But, for a long time, he stood chin deep in the cold water, thinking of relativity and Einstein, and Beatles lyrics, and girls he'd kissed in high school. He thought of guys he'd known in Nam, and, then, he put together an all-star baseball team of Cleveland Indians from the fifties and sixties. He thought of the creature, too. And, eventually, minutes or hours or seconds later, he convinced himself that the thing had truly vanished back into the woods for good and that he was safe to return to shore. He shifted slowly back towards the land.

Joe's next step missed the bottom of the pond and his toe dipped down looking for the sandy bottom again. Again, he missed the bottom, and he treaded closer towards the trees. The moonlight cast across the flat surface of the pond, shimmering clear against the dark water. He saw, now, that the water was dark blue, an aberrant sapphire in a forest of brown, iron-tinged streams, marshes and lakes.

He dropped his legs down again, a sudden feeling of panic gripping him as his feet kicked out again into empty water. Still, no bottom. Though he was closer to the shore and moving back in the same direction he'd come, the lake had somehow grown deeper. "No," he breathed hoarsely. "I turned around somehow." Pinpointed on the wrong tree. He found the moon again and marked the trees, but the surrounding wall of pines now all looked exactly the same.

The water grew colder still, an icy bite that rolled up his legs and back. He hung within the unique nothingness of water, floating in the cold and black water, the darkness itself surrounding him now on all sides. Face wet, his lungs pushed feebly against the unnatural chilly air, and he choked on each hard breath as he swam hard for the shore.

Just below him came the sounds. The low scratching sounds, muted and dawdling at first were so quiet that Joe thought he'd only imagined them. He stilled his breathing, heartbeat thumping in his ears, and listened carefully. Yes, he thought, there was something there. Something scraping, something deliberate. The sound of black nails clawing somehow out of the water towards him. Growing louder, stronger, more angry.

An animal of some kind, he thought, hoped. He'd certainly raked out enough carcasses of turtles and foxes to justify the thought. But the thing that stirred in the darkness just beneath him was not a turtle.

Eventually, he heard words. Rather, sounds much like words that crept along the splashing water and echoed in his very mind. The noise was deep and multi-tonal, at least three separate voices speaking at once, and chillingly familiar. He could make out no phrases, no single word, but as he splashed and struggled towards the shore, he eventually found meaning in the voice.

Only emotions and ideas carried in the dark tones of the reply. *Fear. Doom. Abyss.* The darkness, the water, wanted him.

"Leave me be." Joe groaned. His own words came out as a whisper of frost. "Why won't you just leave me be." He could smell it then. Something foul, rotting in the stillness of the dark pond. It touched him.

A poke at the bottom of his foot. Something like fingers grazed across the top of his boot again, grabbing around his ankle. Like soggy twigs, something rotted and wet to the touch. He shuddered, his sharp cry caught quickly in the night air, and he jerked his foot away again. The ghostly claws simply reached out once more and furiously scratched at his lower leg before vanishing again into the black waters.

Joe's swimming became more frantic. His arms pumped forward, flailing almost, his feet kicking out against the icy water.

Its mouth closed suddenly down upon his lower leg, biting to the bone. Joe screamed, the sound completely filling the blackness around him, and water splashed into his mouth. He kicked out violently, his leg in a spasm of pain. He thought he felt teeth, jagged fangs against his skin, ripping into the muscle, pulling away with strips of skin. Something warm suddenly ran down his foot and Joe knew that it was his own blood. Below, he felt cold pressed against his foot, sucking at the fresh blood that ran from his leg. Feeding on it, slurping sounds mixed against his own shrieks. Just like a mosquito, he thought hazily. Add another bite to the report.

Its mouth, mouths it seemed now, lurched forward again, biting down onto his toes. Joe swam more violently, his entire body floundering to pull away, and his glasses fell away at last into the dark waters. He felt small hands grab hold of his other leg, pulling his foot down towards black jaws. He kicked out again, yanking his feet spastically against the horrible feel of bony nails.

Memories flooded his thoughts, images he'd buried so well until now, hidden from his family and fiancée, even from himself. The blackness below snarled suddenly beneath him. Growled like some wolf from a bedtime story. He felt several heavy forms shift below him, moving closer. Something sharp and icy pushed through the water and latched hold of the sides of his legs. Below, the dark moved once more, and Joe could feel claws sinking into the flesh of his legs again, piercing like nails into his skin.

He looked down, hoping to at least see the creature from the woods perhaps, or some monstrous fish from depths and caves too awful and ancient. Instead, he saw faces in the water. Gnarled and revolting faces like none he'd seen before. The bloated white eyes of some inexpressible horror that hadn't seen daylight in more than a million years. Blearing, shimmering in the water just beside him. Halloween masks. The faces of demons.

He splashed forward, every muscle lurching against the terrible weight of the darkness around him, and swam with all his strength.

Something raked down his back and whether it was some monster's crusty claws or a protruding branch, he didn't know, and he didn't care. He lifted upwards again. The shore some-

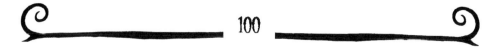

how further away now.

Too tired to swim, he thought grimly, *Drowning . . . .*

Water splashed in his face. He spit the grime out, gritty in his mouth. Eyes fluttering madly. Again, the things struck at him, more claws and daggers tearing into his body. Words and thoughts of such malevolence and dread filled his head again. He quivered in madness, not sure where the shadows of the pond ended and his own dark shape began.

Claws dug into his back, a powerful clutch more sturdy, more real than the others. He found himself being lifted from the water and struggled against the steely grip. He dropped to the ground, wet and trembling on the pond's sandy shore.

"You're all right," a deep voice said.

Joe jerked away from the sound and scooted up on his hands and backside, squinting through haze and murky water. A man stood just above him. He was older, maybe in his sixties, and tall and brawny with graying hair and a short scraggy beard. "What were you thinking?" he asked.

Joe shook away the question, his heart pounding, gasping for air. His hands ran down to his legs, expecting to feel the shreds of bones and flesh that remained. He found his legs in perfect shape, only the one pant leg ripped. "I don't . . ." he turned to the man. "Who are you?"

"Winslow," he pointed backwards. "Abe. Live back that way. Heard something."

"Something," Joe repeated. *The demon's sharp cries. His own frenzied screams, perhaps. The luring call of the demons in the water.* "What? I don't understand."

The man looked back towards the water just a few feet away. "Folk don't swim in that pond," he said. "Never have. Not since before I was a boy."

Joe stood slowly, his legs wobbling. "What's down there?"

The man looked at him, his grin easy, understanding. "Some say demons," he said, shrugging. "Coming up from the very depths of hell."

"Demons." Joe recalled the ghoulish faces he'd seen in the water, his mind already fighting to erase the memory. Like so many memories he'd been erasing. "Demons."

"That pond has no bottom," the man said simply. "It just goes down, well, forever. Down to hell, some figure."

"That's—" Joe stopped himself from finishing the thought as the man glared at him. Shivering on the dark shoreline, anything now seemed possible.

"City folk have come out on boats and tried to find the bottom. Dropped lines with weights and had to get more rope. Still couldn't get to the bottom."

"And that, that thing?" he asked squinting back into the woods. "What do 'some' say about that?"

"You see something out here?" the old man asked, the teasing gleam of a smile in his eye.

Joe shook his head. "I don't know" He stopped, thinking on the evening. "I don't know. I gotta find my jeep."

"First, why don't you come back to the house. Get you a blanket, something to eat. Looks like you had a rough night."

"Yeah," Joe agreed turning back to the dark pond. "Guess you could say that."

The old man studied him for awhile, eyes narrowed in thought. "When I was a boy," Abe Winslow said. "They used to say that those who'd escaped the pond had faced their darkest fears and beaten them."

Joe numbly considered his point. He did feel strangely alive. "I didn't, you pulled me out. I would have drowned otherwise." He saw something in the woods then, a familiar dark shape hunched just across the pond.

Abe Winslow smiled, also looking out over the still water. "Anything wrong with getting a little help?"

"No," Joe admitted slowly, watching the creature. "I guess not. Whatever it takes."

"Some out there, they can't ever lose the demons inside," the old man turned away from the pond, his face half-cast in shadow. "Not ever."

NOTES: The Jersey Devil is said to boil streams with its hot breath to catch the fish within. There are several mysterious "Blue Holes" throughout the Pine Barrens, some more famous and remote than others. Stories hinting that the water holes have no bottom and are filled with monsters go back hundreds of years, and only the bravest locals ever dared, or dare, to swim in such pools. In truth, each water hole has a sandy bottom and is fed by a deep natural spring, so the water is always icier and also "bluer" than the sun-warmed and iron-stained brown water of the Pine Barren's standard creeks and ponds. These curious pools are often linked to the Jersey Devil as preferred bathing or watering holes.

BIRDS OF A FEATHER
1978

The bone was blackened and partially eroded from the elements and fire. Linda leaned closer into the magnifying glass. "It's so decayed," she sighed. "Maybe a proximal wing finger. Nine inches long, which suggests a large bird. Perhaps the wing-tip bone of a large ground-dwelling bird."

"Like a crane?"

Linda glanced at Andy Butler, the watchdog assigned to her for the next two days. The state forester was in his early forties, his tanned and careworn face framed by curly dark hair and a full mustache. He wore jeans and a tan long-sleeve shirt with the New Jersey Division of Parks and Forestry emblem on the right pocket above his name. He seemed pleasant enough, but she could tell clearly he hadn't volunteered for the assignment. "Indeterminate," she replied.

The State had found the partial skeleton—decayed remains of claws, feathers, bone particles, and a hind leg—a month earlier in a cranberry bog that had been swept by fire the previous summer. One of her colleagues at Berkeley had read something about it, the *Death of the Jersey Devil*, and she'd flown out to get a better handle on the legend and the recent discovery as part of their larger project and research.

"Pterosaur wing bones are easily identified as long as they're preserved intact." She shook her head and breathed deeply. "Which, of course, is not the case here." She squinted at the specimen, drawing as heavily as she could on her scant three years of experience in paleontology. "I'm looking for internal cavities and thin bones with a strong outer layer. Here, maybe. No." She frowned. "Let's see that other one again." She reached over to where the remains lay in a metal box. "This one."

She nodded, grabbing a piece with her tongs. "Possibly a pteroid bone. Ran between the pterosaur's wrist and shoulder, supporting part of the wing membrane." She inspected it under the glass and light, her long brown ponytail for once staying put behind her shoulders. "Such a novel structure is rare among vertebrates. Evolution usually co-opts bones from old functions and structures to new ones."

"A pteroid bone?" Andy interrupted her. "You weren't kidding, then."

"Sounds like you're not a big fan of our lost dinosaur theory."

"Sorry," the forester's face creased into a small smile. "No offense. Just seems a little far-fetched is all."

She looked up from the table and raised her brows. "The demon-baby version a little more believable?"

The smile edged toward a grin, and Andy laughed. "Okay, okay," he said. "Fair enough."

"Let me show you something." She stepped across the room and grabbed a book from her backpack. "Dimorphodon," she said, and dropped a book on the table, moving to a page she'd bookmarked. "One of the oldest pterosaurs, before the pterodactyls everyone knows. Lived in the Jurassic period. About five feet long, with wings made of skin and a broad head." She pointed at the book. "Look like anyone you know?"

The illustration showed a birdlike dinosaur, with a disproportionately large head and stubby beak. It looked a little like a horse head. It had massive sinewy bat wings attached to its front arms and stood on its hind legs. A long pointed tail, like that of a cartoon devil, trailed behind.

"Unbelievable," Andy ran his finger across the picture, and Linda nodded, watching him. It might as well have been another picture of the traditional Jersey Devil. "That's dead on."

"We thought so, too," she said. "Pterosaurs had modified epidermal structures that were wing-supporting fibers with hair-like structures to provide insulation. They would have looked to us a little like a big hairy bat with a huge snout. And based on studies of its hips and legs, we think Dimorphodon was one of the few pterosaurs that had an erect, birdlike stance. The legs directly under the body, so that they could run or hop on their toes very quickly." Linda picked up one of the bones again, and mimicked it skipping across the table. "Again, just like your Jersey Devil stories, right?"

"But, dinosaurs still roaming the earth?"

"Why not?" she replied. "Dimorphodon 'roamed' for 250 million years. What's another forty? Maybe the glaciers missed a few. Maybe they somehow survived extinction."

"Living in underground caves and the like."

She nodded. "So you've read your H.G. Wells and Edgar Rice Burroughs."

"My kids like that new *Land of the Lost* show," he smiled back. "Same idea for Loch Ness, right? A trapped dinosaur."

"A plesiosaur, right," she spoke excitedly. "Did you see the pictures in *Nature* magazine a few months back?" He shook his head, and she grinned. "Fantastic! Taken just last year near the bottom of the loch. A flipper or fin they think. Enormous."

"Sounds . . ." Andy's eyes widened. "Wow. Those pictures are real?"

"Not my pictures," she allowed. "But even NASA gave it the thumbs up. In the seventies, the rotting corpse of a twenty-foot creature with a long neck and what appeared to be flippers washed up on the shores of Massachusetts of all places. They still don't know what it is."

"What about that Japanese ship a couple months ago?" he asked.

"You saw that?" She beamed. "Yeah, the *Zuiyo-Maru* netted a thirty footer just off New

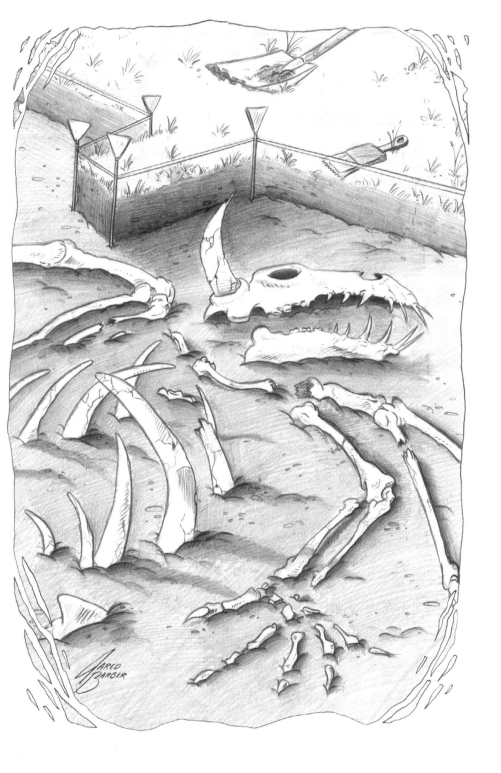

Zealand. Almost four thousand pounds. A globster, they're called. A big glob of unknown animal. The fisherman said it looked just like a turtle that'd crawled out of its shell."

"Then tossed it back into the ocean." He smirked.

Linda grimaced. "Yes, they were more interested in protecting the caught fish from its stench than in any scientific examination. At least they took some pictures and measured it first. Most fossil data suggests plesiosaur died out millions of years ago, but with a lake that deep and seasonal access to the ocean, who knows? We've got a team up in Lake Champlain right now, in fact."

"There's something in that lake?"

"Lake Champlain, Falmouth Bay, Loch Morar, Lake Okanagan, Manitoba. In Argentina's Nahuel Huapi Lake. Turkey. Everyone's got their own plesiosaur swimming about."

"Maybe its just a big sturgeon" he offered.

"Indeterminate." She smiled. "Did you know there's a creature called the Megalania that's been reported by Australian ranchers for more than a hundred years?"

He shook his head. "Sorry."

"A predatory reptile that walks on two legs. Fifteen feet high."

He whistled.

"For hundreds of years, stories have been told of surviving dinosaurs in the jungles of central Africa. The Mokele-Mbembe, for instance."

"Bigfoot?"

"Exactly," Linda agreed. "Bigfoot, yeti, Chinese wildmen, the Yowie in Australia, the Prang-Pendek in Indonesia, the Batutut . . . same thing. These are more than random 'monster' sightings. They are sightings of zoological types identical to species we know to have once existed."

Andy rubbed his jaw, his eyes dropping to the bones again. "Could explain where the dragon stories come from."

"Doesn't it? What makes more sense? That this Leeds creature has lived two hundred years? Or, perhaps, several generations of such creatures, enough to explain centuries of sightings."

"Makes sense, I suppose."

"How about that week in 1909, when it was seemingly spotted forty places at once? Maybe a flock of something had been flushed out of its hiding spot that month."

"What about the feathers," he said indicating the remains in the tray. "Dinosaurs didn't have wings."

"Actually," She shook her head. "There's some ground-breaking work being done now that argues many dinosaurs probably were feathered. And, that, based on bone studies, birds are direct descendents of dinosaurs like the raptor or Pterodactylus. Ever take a good look at a bird's scale-like legs?"

"Meat eaters, too?" he asked, tapping the Dimoradon picture.

"Definitely," she replied. "We think all pterosaurs were carnivores."

Andy nodded again, and glanced over at her. "So, what's the verdict?" he asked.

"Identification is very difficult," she said. "Nothing but bits and pieces and most of those are burnt and decayed. They probably won't do much better back at Berkeley, but it's worth the shot."

"You wanted to see where we found it."

"Pterosaurs lived in small groups." She flipped off the magnifying light. "Cranes, too. If there's one set of remains there, there should be signs, droppings or tracks or remains, of others."

His smile was quick, open. "So you're open to the crane idea."

"Crane. Dimorphodon. A "Linda Blair" baby, perhaps."

The forester laughed and she grabbed her backpack. "I just want to get to the truth," she said.

The Hampton Furnace had remained in operation for more than fifty years, from 1795 to 1850. A hundred years later, all that remained of the once bustling colonial community was scattered building foundations overgrown in bracken fern and sheep laurel. Just behind one of the ancient stone structures, Linda crouched beside the Hampton Creek and finished pouring the plaster into the tracks she'd found.

"Should dry in about thirty minutes," she said, squinting up at the forester. "I suppose you expected hoof prints." She grinned.

"Bird tracks, actually," he replied shielding the sun from his own eyes and looking down at the tracks. "A crane or heron, wouldn't you say?"

"Pterosaurs have three forward-pointing toes and a hallux, the back toe, just like modern birds. The same goes for theropods like the Velociraptor."

"So you can't tell the difference between them?"

"Dimorphodon weighed more than any crane and casts should give us an idea of weight. Plus the length of the back toe changes species to species. That's why I'm not a big fan of the sand hill crane theory. Most of the stories I've found have the Jersey Devil lurking in trees or on window sills. The crane's back toe is simply too short to grip anything. You'll never see a crane in a tree."

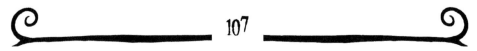

"Never?"

"It'd be a circus-worthy balancing job. A heron's foot could, but not a crane." She stood up and brushed off her jeans. "It's amazing how quickly the trees grew back from a fire."

"Isn't it," he agreed. "Almost every tree in the Barrens tolerates fire and also instinctively sprouts after one. Only three pines in the world can do that, and we've got two of them here."

They walked beside the creek together, looking for more tracks or droppings. "It's quite beautiful out here," she said. "I'm sorry to admit I didn't even know there was a Pine Barrens."

"Few do," he shrugged. "Folk know the turnpikes well enough and maybe the shore and the boardwalk. But few stop to think about what they're driving through when they're on those turnpikes or heading to the shore. A million acres of mostly uninhabited wilderness in the middle of the most densely populated state in the country."

Linda turned toward the flowing creek. "Sounds like the ideal place for an endangered species to settle down and take cover."

"I can't deny that." He laughed, shaking his head. "Pterosaurs ever live in marshes?"

"Most dinosaurs took a stab at marshes and swamplands at one point. We believe the earlier Pterosaurs, like Dimorphodon, preferred the bogs and marshes of prehistoric Earth. It's the later species who liked the cliffs and mountains by the seas. Like the ones we were tracking in Texas when we stumbled upon this 'Jersey Devil' thing."

"The 'Big Bird' you called it, right?" he said, leaning over to check a budding bush.

"That's what the press is calling it," she replied. "Or the *tacuache*. There've been several recent sightings in southern Texas of an unknown flyer with a fifteen-foot wingspan that's been described as a pterodactyl or a giant opossum with wings."

"Media hype," he said. "Tabloid stuff."

Linda listened to the sudden and clear sound of a truck's engine starting in the distance. "Maybe," she said. "But, the America Indians have a long history of encounters with creatures reminiscent of pterosaurs and they weren't trying to sell tee-shirts. The Pima, Hopi, the Yaqui, the Sioux all have stories. Not myth, but actual stories about giant birds they fought that lived in the mountains and grabbed horses and men. In Mexico, they've found Mayan sculptures depicting an animal very similar to a pterodactyl. Missionaries and settlers on both continents called them Thunderbirds . . ." She trailed off, then dropped to one knee to inspect some droppings. "What do herons eat?" she asked. "Or cranes?"

"They're both omnivores. Seeds, grain, berries, insects, mice, smaller birds—"

"Snakes?" she asked examining the specimen. Inside the droppings were the definite spine bones of a small snake.

"Whatever they can get their beaks on."

As a new truck pulled up towards them, she finished scooping the specimen into a plastic bag and dropped it into her backpack with other samples she'd collected.

Another forester, a stout crew-cut man in sunglasses, got out of his truck and joined them. Andy introduced him as Scott Fisher. "Any luck?" the man asked.

Linda ignored the implied mockery in his voice. "Yes, thank you," she said.

"I heard you guys were out here," he said turning to Andy. "Found one of those deer again. Thought you'd like a look."

Linda's eyes widened. "What's that?"

"Thanks, Scott." Andy sighed. He glanced back at the paleontologist. "Every so often a deer turns up. We find a carcass or some hunter bags a buck that's been scratched up pretty bad. Claw marks."

"Interesting." She smiled, looking at Andy. "Cranes ever attack deer?"

"No," he replied. "But, cougars do. Bobcats too. We got 'em both out here."

"Thanks for the tip," she said to the second forester.

Scott smiled, his brows waggling behind his shades. "You should take her out on one of your Devil hunts," Fisher offered, grinning at Andy.

"What's this now?" Linda led them back to the last cast she'd made.

"Andy's been known to drive out at night," Scott continued against Andy's slowly shaking head. "And he looks for, he grinned again, "well, you know."

"The Jersey Devil." She contained her own smile.

"There are a couple spots I like to stop at some nights." Andy wiped his brow. "But it's not just a couple of spots where, where you sometimes see things."

"And where exactly might that be?" Linda asked, pulling out a map of the park.

Andy shook his head again, his sigh deeper this time. "I thought you might say something like that."

The next night, Linda sat alone on the hood of the truck the Forest Service had lent her, stoically watching one of the locations Andy had suggested. The night air rolled cool over the murky bog. She warmed her arms while staring into the dark marshland as the buzz of night insects and frogs filled her ears and the moon drifted out of the clouds to run a shaft of ghostlight over the grass waving ominously just ahead.

Her last day had been spent vigorously scouting various locations throughout the park and collecting samples of nests, droppings and more casts of prints. The morning's autopsy of the fresh deer carcass suggested a midsized feline, and Linda shot three roles of film while peppering Andy Butler with a hundred questions on the Barrens and the wildlife found within. Three hundred species of birds dwelled within the dark pines, and an assortment of bears, foxes and bobcats. The single hoof print she'd found near Batsto was explained by Andy as weekend equestrians.

A hoof print, she groaned, thinking of the other possibility. "Absurd," she mumbled to herself, and the noise of her own voice proved quite startling in the untamed Pines. The night before, she'd found a small bookstore in town and picked up the seminal book on the Jersey Devil myth. The blood-red book featured a picture of the creature on the front, a beastly dragon hovering over a forest of dark pines beneath. Still looks like a pterosaur to me, she declared, thinking about hoofed feet and scanning the tall trees just behind her. "Absurd," she said again, half-wondering how less absurd a surviving flock of Dimorphodon might be.

Across the way, she suddenly made out a figure in the high scrub of the bog. An outline she hadn't noticed before now stood among the reeds, the long black shadows from the surrounding trees casting unusual lines of darkness across the peculiar shape. Her stomach knotted into a tight ball.

The shadowed thing stood maybe six feet tall, though hunched over some above the water. It turned, moving slowly in the dark with the fluid motion of a lizard. Etched black in the moonlight, it slowly stepped towards her, and she reached for the unlit flashlight at her side. She made out what appeared to be a tail and wings. It took another step forward, and its lengthened and distorted shadow stretched across the bog and fell upon the truck.

It walked on two legs, like a man, stepping through the water with low slushing sounds. All other noises in the Barrens had stopped, the nocturnal calls of insects and frogs long since vanished. The shape's head was long and sharp, thrust forward, and the red of the animal's eyes shimmering suddenly in the moon's light.

Linda's heart rattled in her chest as she moved carefully across the hood and slid off the side of the truck. Something other than a bobcat had killed that deer, she realized, swallowing. And, whether it was a living dinosaur or . . . or something else, that no longer mattered. She brought the flashlight up, thumb poised on the switch to turn it on, and pointed it at the thing.

The shape moved again, immense wings extending out behind its crooked dark shape. Seven-foot wingspan. She shuddered. No, at least eight. She flipped on the flashlight and light pushed at last into the dark bog.

The sound that filled the forest then was like nothing she'd ever heard before. It was a shrill howl, garbled and snarling, and she instinctively brought her hands to her ears, her flashlight's beam swooshing up into the night sky.

Garoo-a-a-a-a-! The cry ratcheted up higher still, the echo of the strange call running through the dark forest. The shriek warbled, ending finally in rough throttling noise.

Linda's hand trembled as she bought the flashlight around again and pointed it back towards the marshland.

Now the creature skulked just behind the marsh grass, half-cast in night shadow. She made out long ash grey legs and an elongated neck. It was covered in course brown hair, and swamp grass and mud dripped from its grotesque and massive wings. Enormous digits extended out from the wings, long fingers growing off the tips. The face gleamed red up top, sharp fangs glistening in the faint, quivering light. She fell against the side of the truck, reaching for the door.

The thing stepped forward again, and Linda screamed.

Something moved beside her suddenly, and she felt claws digging into her arm, pulling her away from the truck. She swung the flashlight towards the thing but it caught her in mid-swing. "Linda," it shouted at her. "It's okay. It's me. Andy."

She opened her eyes completely for the first time since the thing's cry and stared up at the forester. A string of curse words she hadn't learned in science class filled the next few moments between them.

"What!" she half shouted at him finally. "What is it?"

Andy Butler reached past her into the truck. "*Grus Canadensis,*" he said. The truck's headlights flooded the bog suddenly. "The sandhill crane."

The bird stood blinking in the headlights. It was tall and stately with a heavy tear-shaped body, a long neck and slender legs. The eyes glistened black above a lengthy, razor-sharp bill. The wings dropped back to its sides, the staggered feathers laying back into place. She'd only imagined its weight, adding pounds because of its height and the night's shadows. The bird probably weighed no more than twenty pounds.

It turned sideways, and Linda got a good view of its bill, tapering down to a sharp point and the rusty red tinge just above its eyes. The feathers were matted and dirty, covered in dried mud, and as it darted jerkily away from the light back into the night, it vanished completely.

"Thought I'd come up and see how you were doing," the forester said quietly behind her. "Glad I did."

"Thanks so much," she snapped and tossed the flashlight back into the truck. "You set me up."

"You wanted to see something," he said, shrugging. "Don't see cranes out here much, but when I have, this is a good spot."

"A mutant crane, maybe," she huffed. "That thing was like no bird I've ever seen."

"They smear mud on their wings for camouflage and to repel parasites."

She breathed deeply, pushing out any remaining fear. "Dinosaurs did that too."

He looked over the bog. "The sandhill's call can be heard from over ten miles away. Remarkably loud and penetrating thanks to an unusual windpipe." He turned to her and drew a picture in the air. "They've got an elongated trachea forming a single loop which fills the cavity in the sternum."

"I thought," she gulped. "I thought it was . . ."

"And you were out here looking for cranes and pterosaurs. Imagine what the first settlers must have thought when they saw one of those birds hopping about? Most quite new to the mysterious dark continent and none of them sensible scientists. Heck, imagine what a camper would think if he saw one now."

"I think I can." She shook her head. "I was surprised it kept coming at me. The flashlight didn't seem to scare it at all."

"They're quite aggressive, actually," he said. "With that eight-inch-long bill, they're said to poke straight through a man's head."

"First, that's disgusting. Second, it sounds a bit like local story telling to me." She smiled. "But, of course, that's your point."

"I didn't mean to scare you."

"Yeah, you did," she grimaced. "But, that's okay. You've earned it, I suppose. I guess I should just be glad it wasn't your buddy, Scott, in a devil outfit."

He shook his head. "I read that several conger eels were recently dumped in Loch Ness by some fisherman hoping to add to the hype."

"I saw that too," she said. "One measured over seven feet long."

"I wouldn't do that," he said, looking at her. "I'm as interested in the truth as the next guy. Whether that happens to be a pterodactyl or a heron or, or something else. So be it. That's good enough for me."

Linda nodded, looking over the marsh. "Me, too."

Andy Butler, a veteran of the New Jersey Division of Parks and Forestry, sat quietly in his truck overlooking one of his favorite spots again. A preferred watering hole. One of the many locations he hadn't told the paleontologist about.

Waiting in the dark now, he felt a little guilty about sending the girl out on a wild goose chase—or a wild-crane chase, he mused—but it had been for her own good. She wasn't going to find the flying dinosaurs she was looking for. *She might have found something else, though.*

But, now she was safely back in California, the research done, and her grant money pointed back to Texas.

Andy had figured the new book would bring attention again to the area. It had already brought several journalists, out-of-state thrill seekers, and more than a handful of serious sci-

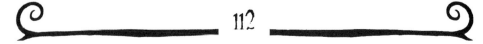

entist—scientists with cameras, night vision, and field kits. How long before things like satellites and DNA-testing were used by the same group, those in search of the truth? And, how long could a million acres keep 'em all guessing?

A long time, Andy decided again watching the dark shape step fully into the moonlight. A long time indeed.

He stared ahead, holding his breath, his hands up under his chin in wonder.

Just across the stream, the Jersey Devil leaned forward to drink.

NOTES: "Eerie bones" were found by the New Jersey Department of Conservation and Economic Development in Hanover in 1956. They were never identified. The rest of the monsters in this story and their sightings are real, though the "globsters" of Massachusetts later proved to be, as most globsters do, the decayed body of a shark. The Loch Ness shots were revealed as fakes in 1990, as was the infamous Bigfoot film we all know. The thunderbirds of Texas and South America, as well as the Jersey Devil, remain unexplained.

FRIGHT NIGHT
1986

I hate Halloween.

Not exactly a new thought to Frank Spanelli. He hadn't cared much for any of the ghost or goblin crap when he was a kid either, everyone telling stupid stories and morons yelling "Boo" at the top of their lungs. He and his brother usually just tossed on their Little League uniforms and went as ball players. Nothing wrong with free candy.

Now, a decade later, Trooper Spanelli cruised down highway 532, skirting the north end of the Wharton State Forest, and again confirmed his childhood assessment. Earlier in the night, he'd driven past the houses and stores decorated with blanketed ghosts swinging loosely from trees and cardboard cutouts of witches and skeletons. Jack-o-lanterns rested cold and dead on porches and front steps, the candles inside, long since blown out. A lone black cat, hunched low against wind, slithered along the top of a split rail fence. And, behind all the hooey, was another Halloween night of prank calls, childish vandalism, and drunken bar fights. All this, and not a single Snickers bar in sight.

He checked his watch, 1:14 am. The two-lane road remained empty. With Medford twenty minutes behind, his cruiser's headlights sliced through a line of pitch black night Above, the stars were bright in the cold sky, the full moon dipping back into the black pines.

Spanelli grunted and reached for the radio dial. Despite Barclay's valiant efforts, the Sixers had just lost by a dozen to the Lakers. "Should have thought about that before you traded away Malone and Daugherty." Spanelli shook his head as the dark wall of trees passed on either side of his car. Whenever the Phillies or Sixers visited the West Coast, the car's radio could kill the first couple hours of night shift pretty well—which was crucial. In the winter, there were nights he'd go hours without seeing another car, sometimes, it was all night.

Spanelli sighed deeply and slowed to turn onto a narrow dirt road marked only with a small green sign that read St 4235. He turned down the game to call back the barracks. "Tom River, Two-William-Thirty," he spoke into his mic as the forest swallowed his car fully, trees filling in both sides of his view. Total darkness fell in behind him in the afterglow of his car lights.

"Two-William-Thirty, clear." A static-riddled voice hissed over the state police radio. He brought the car to a crawl, moving only another hundred yards into the woods. Way too easy to get stuck in the sand back here.

Spanelli stopped the car. "Two-William-Thirty on site." Some joker had called through one of the turnpike phones, something about kids needing help and screaming in the woods. *Kids screaming on Halloween, imagine that.* The anonymous caller even gave the old road off 532.

"Local backup in route, Two-William-Thirty."

Whatever. "I'm gonna take a walk around and see if I can find 'em."

"Clear, Two-William-Thirty," the dispatcher came back.

Spanelli kept the headlights on and climbed out of the car. He wore dark blue slacks and a French blue jacket, the famed state trooper mountie hat rested smartly on his crew-cut head. The fall air was crisp, but certainly reasonable for one thirty in the morning.

The black trees ran fifty acres deep on each side in the Wharton tract, and he could only see a few steps into the forest with his flashlight. He hoped the kids had already taken off, but he rarely had that kind of luck.

Couldn't see much, but he heard them clear enough. Sounded like a small group, at least one girl, and the voices weren't too far off the path. He reached into the car and grabbed the mic again. "Toms River, Two-William-Thirty."

"Two-William-Thirty, clear."

"They're still out here. How's that local comin', Toms River?"

"ETA, fifteen minutes," the dispatcher replied.

Isn't Halloween technically over? He sighed. "I'm heading back there now," he informed.

"One thirty-four a.m. Two-William-Thirty, clear."

He moved towards the voices with steady steps and with the flashlight held up as he stepped into the opening. His expectation was the typical teenage party in the woods. But, unlike his other Halloween prejudices, this one was not borne out.

Two shapes crouched in the darkness, a third standing above them as Frank focused his beam on the entire group. "State Police," he barked.

The figures remained almost motionless as he looked around the rest of the opening. "Who else is out here?" he shouted at them. "What you got there?"

The three, all in their teens, stared blankly at him, their faces squinting into his light. Each wore dark eye makeup and had painted their faces. The girl was crouched down by one of the boys, the other one just standing there, looking lost. The boy on the ground was sniffling, and they all looked scared.

"Halloween's over, gang. You okay?" he asked the girl looking around again. She nodded, saucer eyes swiveling back towards him. She wore black stretch pants and a cheap black witch cloak, her hair Aqua-Netted into a coif that would have made Jon Bon Jovi applaud.

The opening had been cleared to bare ground and two dozen unlit candles peppered the area. Spanelli also saw what looked liked a Ouija board and a pack of cards spilled in the dirt. A deep rut in the ground ran around the whole opening in a wide ring, a perfect circle.

"Stand up," he told them, and they did so quietly. "Park's closed," he grunted. "Your parents know you're out here?"

"Yeah," the boy who'd been standing replied.

Spanelli put the light directly in the kid's face. "Name?"

"Brian."

"Brian what?"

"Kaechele." Even his lips were painted black. He was a tall, thin kid with a lousy complexion and a curly shoulder-length mullet. He wore a necklace with a poker-chip sized pentagram around his neck. Great, he thought, another warlock from Spencer's Gifts.

"Where you live, Brian Kaechele?"

"Cherry Hill."

Spanelli dropped the light some. "Where you guys parked?"

"They took off." The girl said, her voice shaking. "They—" She stopped, and Spanelli caught the look that passed between her and young Brian Kaechele.

"What's wrong with you?" he asked the smaller kid. "You hurt or something?" The boy, a chubby-faced kid a couple years younger than the other two, looked at his friends. "What's your name, pal?" Spanelli prompted him.

"Lee . . . Lee Reiner."

"So what, you guys Motley Crue for Halloween or something?"

"Yeah," the first kid said, too quickly. "Halloween. Stupid, huh?"

"Grab your stuff," he rejoined and waved them to follow him out of the clearing, but only the little one moved, a nervous little stutter step. "Move out," he ordered again.

The three teenagers shifted slightly, but hadn't come any closer.

"Hey, gang. Not for discussion."

They looked at each other, eyes wide. "We can't," the girl said finally, her words barely a whisper.

Spanelli grimaced. Kids. "Let's not make this worse, okay? You guys are already in big trouble."

"She's right," Brian said hesitantly. "We can't follow you."

"Brian, it's been a long night, and I ain't gonna argue with a guy in makeup. Move you butt."

"But, we can't leave the circle," the second boy said quietly, and Brian and the girl's eye widened even more.

"What?" The officer looked down briefly, and realized his boots were currently standing on the deep line forming the circle in the center of the clearing. "You three escaped loonies or something?"

"It's a magic circle," the girl explained. "For . . ."

116

"Casting," Lee completed with authority. "Casting spells."

Spanelli tapped the flashlight on his thigh. "I . . ." he stopped, trying to marshal his response. Halloween. Somewhere along the line his head had started throbbing, and he wondered some how Charles Barclay and the Sixers would handle their next game out on the coast. No use. Sighing, he glanced at the teenagers. "The black magic thing, huh? Light some candles and read a couple poems about vampires, right? Bet you guys play Dungeons and Demons too."

"Dungeons and Dragons," the smaller kid corrected.

Spanelli groaned. "Backup'll be here in about two minutes, and then you're all leaving 'the circle' one way or the other. 'Other' includes fun things like probation and court dates. So let's go." He waved them on again, hoping for the best.

"We can't leave the circle," the girl repeated and this time, he could see that she was about to cry. "We just can't."

"Sure didn't stop your friends."

"They ran before it truly formed," she said.

"What's your name?" Spanelli stomped back towards them.

"Kim."

He waited.

"Mason."

"Before what truly formed, Ms. Mason?"

She looked away from his bothered gaze.

"Lee?" he asked, still looking at the girl.

The boy's head dropped. "The Jersey Devil," he said.

"It wasn't the Jersey Devil," Brian hissed.

Spanelli laughed. It was short and it was angry, but it was still a laugh by most accounts.

"You don't believe us," the girl said, looking at him.

The Jersey Devil? Frank Spanelli shook his head again. The other troopers sometimes talked up the stupid monster for the new guys. Some kind of bat thing flying about the Pines and gobbling up little old ladies. An okay hockey team, Spanelli supposed. But you might as well be another moron yelling "Boo" on Halloween. "Brian?"

"Yeah."

"Start talking." He looked back, waiting for backup. Let the local boys drag these three idiots out, he thought.

The kid sighed, shoulders slumping in a pout. "We were gonna summon the Jersey Devil, the Leeds Devil."

"Halloween, midnight," Lee explained.

"Got it," Spanelli smirked. "Then what?"

Brian Kaechele dropped his head, and Spanelli turned to the girl. "There were seven of us," she said. "Billy's sister drove us all, but they took off when it happened."

He waited.

"The spirit, you know? It appeared. We lit the candles and held hands and tried to use the Ouija board, but it wouldn't work. And, then Glenn read some verse from the *Necronomicon*. And we all started, you know, chanting."

Spanelli readjusted his trooper hat and looked out into the dark woods. "To, um, to summon the Jersey Devil," he said.

"Its spirit," the girl amended. "Glenn and Brian don't believe it's a real creature anymore. Not like Big Foot is, I mean. It's more of a lost spirit that, like, still roams the pines. So we did a séance to attract the ghost of the Leeds' thirteenth child."

"The worlds of the living and the dead become blurred on Halloween," Brian said quietly. "*Samhain*, the Celts called it. The costumes and makeup began as a way to trick the ghosts into thinking you were one of them so they'd leave you alone. So we thought we'd try it out, and call the Jersey Devil. But, something happened," Brian muttered. "Something else was drawn to our circle."

"The guys back at the barracks are gonna love you three, really." Spanelli shook his head. "I don't like you at all, of course, but they're really gonna love this."

"Whatever," the girl snapped. "Laugh. I know what I saw."

"Then, for the record," Spanelli led. He didn't bother taking out his notebook.

"I dunno. The candles started to blow, like, funny. The flames got bigger even though there's not much wind. And, I got, like, real cold all of a sudden. Freezing cold, you know?"

"We all did," Lee said.

"That's when Donna started freaking out, screaming about evil spirits and stuff," she continued. "And, Glenn was yelling at her to just shut up. I think most of us just wanted to get up and leave right then."

"Speak for yourself," said Brian.

Kim turned back to Spanelli. "But no one got up. No one broke the hand grasp, and Michelle and Glenn kept saying some weird stuff and then . . . and then I saw it. The candle lights, like, joined and got weird. Like when you squint your eyes at the sun, you know?"

"You guys been drinking?" He saw no such evidence.

"No," she sighed. "We just . . . never mind."

"Go on. I want to get to the part where your friends ditch you and then disturb my evening with an anonymous phone call."

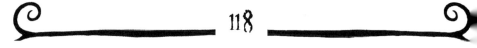

"I didn't see it so good, sir," Lee admitted.

"What about you?" he asked Brian. The boy shrugged, and Spanelli put the flashlight in his face again for good measure. "Back to you Ms. Mason."

She rolled her eyes. "The candle light merged somehow. It became, I don't know, like one long flame, or a golden-blue glow. Right there," she pointed. "In the center and took on a bigger shape. One of the guys was pulling a joke, right? Some kinda, like, fireworks trick or something. But, everyone let go then, and one of the girls started screaming again. That's when it really took shape."

"Took shape?"

"The light got taller, got more the form of something, the shape of something you could, like, almost recognize. The shape of a man."

"Then everyone was screaming," Lee said. "I mean everyone. And they all jumped up and ran back towards the cars."

"But you three stayed?"

Lee shrugged. "We didn't want to leave the circle."

"Nice friends you got. So now, if you—"

"Step out of the magic circle, it can get us. It'll try to kill or possess us or something, Lee finished the sentence for Spanelli."

"Then, that thing's chasing your friends, right? Once they left the circle? He's probably halfway to Marlton by now. Safe to follow me, I bet."

"No," the girl whispered. "Its shape grew clearer still until you could see it almost. A shadow in a flashlight, you know? It . . . the ghost, like, looked at us. Its eyes looked past the costume and makeup and right into me. Black eyes, miserable eyes. Then it floated off into the woods. A glowing mist in the shape of a man." Kim's eyes trailed her words and the memory over Spanelli's shoulder into the black and silent forest just behind him.

"But it wasn't the Jersey Devil," Brian said again.

"That distinction seems important to you, Brian," Spanelli sighed. "What's the deal?"

"He had a fifty-dollar bet with Glenn that the séance couldn't make the Jersey Devil appear."

Brian grunted. "So unless the Jersey Devil wears glasses and a Hawaiian shirt . . . ."

"That's what this 'glowing mist' looked like?"

"Hard to say exactly," the girl said. "But, I guess I saw the same thing. A fat guy with long curly hair and glasses. Like John Lennon glasses, you know? And yeah, definitely, one of those crazy flower shirts."

"Sounds like your pals gave you three a pretty good scare tonight."

"It wasn't a trick," she replied.

Spanelli began to say something, something flavored with just the right touch of derision, when he saw it.

There was a dark outline in the trees, a man watching them. No, he reconsidered. Not a man. His flashlight fell on the shape, and the thing jerked further back into the dark shadows.

He caught a glimpse of dark hair and a pointed head. Some kind of animal. There'd been stories for years about various escaped panthers and lions lose in the Barrens. People finding mutilated dogs and deer and the like. Spanelli's right hand dropped to his sidearm.

"What did you see?" Lee gasped, eyes wide.

He ignored the boy and called out into the woods, "State Police!" Not much good if it turned out to be a panther. He turned angrily at the others. "Your little game is gonna end up getting someone shot."

"That wasn't our friends," the girl murmured.

"No?" He stepped towards the moving shape, aware his next step would pull him outside the circle's boundary. The "magic" circle, he thought, wincing. He stepped just beyond the line and then stopped.

The flashlight cut a path through the black trees and underbrush as something large moved just beyond the reach of the sharp beam. "Identify yourself," he called out. "Or clear out." *Let the idiots run back into the woods, because I ain't taking another step until backup shows. Then, we can arrest each and every one of the brats. Disturbing the peace, trespassing, open fire without a permit, and some other stuff I'll think of later.*

A scream filled the woods. It was an odd, shrill cry, and it sent a chill even down Frank Spanelli's back as the teenagers noisily collapsed in a small heap behind him. His fingers wrapped around his pistol, suddenly wanting to draw the weapon. But too many kids running around playing games—too easy to shoot some guy in a gorilla suit.

The scream had been human, or at least something mostly human, and it surely sounded like something in pain. *What if some punk had really gotten hurt?* As the woods rustled with the shape's moving bulk again, he decided to give chase.

"Don't move," he snapped, turning to the others. He laughed gruffly, "Look who I'm tellin', right?"

He moved slowly, stepping carefully over the fall underbrush with only his flashlight. He'd decided to keep the pistol in its holster for now. The light fell on a shape again, definitely something alive and big moving through the trees. He wondered if he were just chasing a deer, but the way it moved seemed odd. It almost seemed to stop when he did, waiting for him to follow. He walked maybe another hundred yards into the woods and stopped.

"That's enough," he huffed and cast a wide beam around the pitch black forest. In a break between the trees, he found it again.

It stood between two dark pines, a squat little man with jagged wings and the face and snout of a German Shepherd. Spanelli swallowed. "This is nuts," he muttered.

He watched it for a long while, trying to make sense of what his eyes were telling him. A faint blue glow backlit the dark figure and shimmered just behind its movements. Spanelli thought he saw a tail of some kind behind the shape, swaying slowly back and forth across the ghostly light. Pistol drawn now, he stepped closer.

It squawked at his second step, and Trooper Spanelli froze, gun aimed. The thing turned then, hopping away from him like some great sea bird. Spanelli squinted, tracking it. He'd certainly seen herons and cranes in the marshes before. *Was that what this was?* He clearly saw the wings, the hairy wings, as it lifted away from his beam and into the trees. *A heron with hairy wings and the face of a dog?* The creature vanished entirely into the blackened treetops, shadows and full branches swallowing the flashlight's trail.

In the beast's path, unseen branches groaned, and twigs crunched, falling to the dark forest floor. Spanelli stepped slowly after it, closer to the strange light that had remained behind.

He moved nearer still and saw that the light emanated just behind a natural hill in the forest floor. It was a short mound overgrown with fern and wool grass. Just behind it, something actually glowed. The glimmering flared briefly, a clear crackle of blue and white light. Then, he saw someone within the light. A shape entirely human flared within his sight for only a moment. The next, he was already convinced he hadn't seen anything at all and stepped closer towards the mound itself.

The light just ahead diminished, darkening with each step he took. The trees creaked above him, their thick arms reaching over him and blocking out the moon. Heart thumping, he stepped onto the mound itself.

The light disappeared completely, a brief flash of brilliance that washed out in a spreading cloud into the darkness. The woods fell utterly dark again.

He stopped, and his flashlight cut down into the space just behind the rise. Spanelli managed a small, sad smile.

The body sprawled on the forest floor was decayed by time and the elements, and he figured it had been laying in the pines for a dozen years at the very least. Nothing remained but decomposed and moldy strips of clothing, splintered and framed with greyed bone. He saw pieces of washed out red fabric, and the worn and faint pattern of flowers. He cast the flashlight's beam on the skull directly.

The faded skull lay half sunken in the ground, and the back was open with two golfball-sized holes. One of the lower jaw bones was missing, probably dragged off by some raccoon a decade before. Spanelli circled until the skull's dark and lonely eye sockets stared back at him. A pair of glasses, rounded just like the kind John Lennon used to wear, lay just beside.

He looked back into the woods, towards where the first creature had run off. Some zit-faced kid in a costume, the demon dog, the . . . whatever it was. He heard only the mild creak-

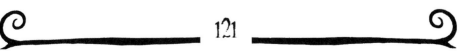

ing and rustles of an ancient forest.

He marked the location and moved quickly back towards the others. Spanelli found them sitting together still, quiet, and exhausted—worn out from fear.

"Get up," he said, and the three got to their feet quickly. "Let's go," he said again, and there was an extra something in his voice, this time, that was somehow more threatening than the loss of the magic circle or some vengeful spirit. They followed closely on his booted heels.

"What was it?" Lee asked breathlessly just behind him. "We heard something"

"You heard nothing. Now move."

The kids fell completely silent behind him as they reached his car. Ahead, he saw the lights of another car. The local sheriff arriving at last. "Thanks, pal," he snorted and opened his door to grab his radio.

"You three. Just stand there and keep quiet. And, unless you want to spend the next few months working with counselors and shrinks, you might want to rethink your ghost and zombie routine."

"I told you," Brian hissed at the others.

Spanelli looked briefly at Brian. "And, you owe your pal Glenn, fifty bucks," he said.

"I . . ."

The other kids' eyes widened, and Spanelli turned away to get to his radio. "Toms River, Two-William-Thirty.".

"Two-William-Thirty, clear."

"Local on site. But, we're going to need a detective and Crime Scene Unit out here now. Got a body. Repeat, found a dead body."

"Is that a body, Two-William-Thirty?"

"Affirmative. Nothin' but bones left. Looks like the guy got shot. And, I think . . ."

"Repeat Two-William-Thirty."

"I . . ." *and I think I saw the Jersey Devil. Might have seen the dead man's ghost too.* "Nothing."

"Will contact detective and CSU."

"Clear."

"Hey, Spanelli, you all right?" The dispatcher asked.

"Yeah, yeah," he replied slowly into the mic, and looked away from the kids who were watching him with confused eyes. "Just . . . just been a weird night is all."

"Gotta love Halloween," the dispatcher laughed tiredly over the radio. "You just gotta love it."

"Affirmative," Officer Spanelli replied quietly. "Two-William-Thirty, clear."

NOTES: Colonel H. Norman Schwarzkopf served as the first commanding officer of the New Jersey State Police, which began active service with eighty-one troopers in 1921. Trained at Sea Girt, New Jersey, the troopers patrolled on horseback and motorcycle. For many of the smaller towns in and around the Pine Barrens, the State Police continue to provide the bulk of law enforcement and surveillance duty. The desolate Pines are not unfamiliar to organized crime and the occasional dumped "problem." Teenagers, and others, interested in Black Magic and the Jersey Devil have been gathering in the pines since the 1960s and their activity increased with the publication of the popular *The Jersey Devil* book. Extra troopers are on duty each Halloween.

THE JERSEY DEVIL CLUB
2004

Kevin Harris joined the Jersey Devil Club over the grilled Reuben special at the Silver Coin diner in Hammonton just a few hours before midnight. It was only a temporary membership, but if it covered him for the next four hours, he didn't care. Just so long as he got the picture he needed.

The group's founder, a thirty-something zoologist from Trenton State named Poppy Dodson, sipped at her coffee and talked energetically with several other members at the long table. The night had so far brought out eight hunters: Luke Mabry and his wife Jenny; a twenty-something postal worker named Dana; three college students from Rutgers University named A.J., Jerry and Bonnie; and a man in his sixties they all called Johnny B. They were waiting on one more.

Kevin drank his coffee and listened as the gang buzzed about the latest Jersey Devil gossip. Nodding with apparent interest, he adjusted his hand so he could easily see his watch. They needed to get to it. He'd allotted one night for Pine Barrens photos for his client, a publisher printing a book on American folklore. "For atmosphere," they'd told him. And, atmosphere he could do. He just didn't want to be all night about it.

Still, the gossip wasn't half bad. Several tires were slashed in Parksville just the weekend before, and something about strange tracks found nearby. Johnny B. announced that he'd done some more research at the Camden County Historical Society and found several new clippings from the infamous week of 1909. The white-haired man handed out the copies he'd promised and then passed an extra over to Kevin's son.

Alex, practiced sidekick that he was, studied the page with a respectful amount of interest and then set it aside carefully to finish his burger and fries. Kevin tousled the boy's hair and smiled. Hyped on Mountain Dew and the possibility of finding the actual Jersey Devil, the eight-year-old was making it through the "boring stuff" pretty darn well.

At first, the group had been alarmingly skeptical of including his youngest son in the night's search. Poppy had even pulled Kevin aside and politely reminded him of the dangers, mostly of those inherent in all woodland outings. She hinted at other possibilities, too. What if this was the night they ran into the Jersey Devil head on? There'd been close calls before, she told him. Definitely something had been watching them on several hunts, following them. There'd been strange tracks one night, and stranger sounds another. And, there'd been many times an overwhelming sense of fear had filled each of them. More than one had cried from fear, and several members, both men and women, had quit altogether and never gone on another hunt.

Kevin listened gravely, then explained that Alex had gone with him on location before, including trips to Canada to photograph bear and a trip out west for a book on snakes. Following his photographer father into odd territory and looking for scary characters was certainly nothing new to the kid. In a moment of brilliance, while waiting for the others to arrive, Alex had also asked Poppy several insightful, borderline precocious, questions about Quaker traditions and the notion of the Jersey Devil as a violent character through the ages.

She hadn't brought up the issue of his involvement again.

He glanced up from his son to see the others looking at him. "My introduction?" Kevin put down his coffee. "I already bored Poppy with this story, but sure, okay. I was a Boy Scout, and we camped at this place called Pine Hill a lot. You know it? Yeah, well, this scout master from another troop introduces us to the main myth and then tells us this demon can take the form of any living creature, even another person."

"That's mentioned, I think, but not truly part of the myth," Dana interjected. Kevin had already pegged her as a fundamentalist of the McCloy and Miller books. Anything that had been printed beyond the scope of those texts met with "scholarly" suspicion.

"I'm just telling you what I heard," he held up his hands in surrender and offered a slight smile. "So the scout master then tells us that years before, the Jersey Devil had showed up at some camp one dark night disguised as a damned Boy Scout. Bloodbath ensues, right? Merit badges and intestines flying everywhere."

The table chuckled and Alex looked up from his Game Boy to prove he'd noticed the curse word.

"So, here I am, sitting around a campfire with another troop we've never met before. Thirty new faces leering in and out of the campfire, moving about the camp. None of us slept a wink that night. Not a wink." Kevin smiled. "I can still picture this one shape, you know, after we'd all gone back to the tents. This silhouette standing just outside the fire's glow, strange blue light playing up behind it somehow. A boy's long shadow somehow stretching all the way down and across our tents. Probably some Eagle Scout taking a quick leak, right?"

"Maybe you're about to find out," Poppy smiled and turned to greet someone who'd just entered the diner.

A stout-figured guy in a long black leather jacket introduced himself as Randy and apologized for being late again. He had a shaved head, square glasses and a short peroxided goatee. "You the photographer dude," he said.

"I am. You must be the tech guy?"

Randy smiled broadly. "Step outside, my friend."

Kevin picked up the bill for the table and the group, Alex in close tow, and followed Randy out into the night and the diner's parking lot. His van, a rusted-out Volkswagen bus, was parked next to Poppy's jeep, and he was already passing gear out to the others.

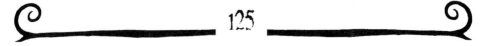

"Here you go, dude," Randy handed Alex a small pair of binoculars. "UNITECH V3s," he said looking up at Kevin. "Built in IR Illuminator, forty LP rez. Nice. Just a hundred bones on Ebay. Sturdy enough for the little man. I've got four of the B12s now." He indicated those who'd gotten those night vision binoculars. "Then, we got these two." He pulled out a case and revealed the goggles inside. "Even with the face mask, weighs less than a pound. Sweet, huh? Operating range is 150 meters, field of view forty degrees. High optics, high." He closed the case again and handed it to Poppy. "Here." He handed Kevin a walkie talkie. "Seven mile radius, even out here." Kevin noticed that each of them had been handed a radio. "Channel 13," Randy beamed, dropping his jacket into the back of the van.

Thirteen, cute. Kevin caught the joke. The thirteenth child. "That GPS?" he asked, pointing to a band around the young man's arm. "Like the joggers use?"

"GPS, yeah. Gotta know where you are, right? Also got wireless, but that's kinda funny out in the Pines, you know. Comes and goes. Hooks right into the armband and sends all data straight back to the van." He pointed up at some unseen satellite and then tapped the pocket-pc purse hanging around his neck. "Takes pics or video. I'll burn disks for everyone with what we got as soon as we get back."

"Yeah," Kevin agreed. "I like to keep a laptop on hand, myself, so I can see the shots. I'll know right away if the lighting isn't working, or if I need to take more."

"Cool," Randy nodded. "Here, check this out." He pulled out what looked like a laser gun with a wide dish on the tip. "Electronic listening dish," he explained. "Got a real tight frequency controller. Just plug in the headphones, aim and shoot, and you get a whisper or footfall from 600 feet away." He handed the listening gun to the college girl, Bonnie.

"Bought with half of a nine-hundred-dollar grant" Poppy said, walking up to them. "The rest is us."

"School's aren't interested yet?" asked Kevin.

"As myth and Jersey folklore, a little. As cryptozoology, no way. Might as well seek grants to find the Easter Bunny. Someday, maybe. With some real focus and real money, who knows what we'll turn up. For now, we're still on our own out here."

Randy huffed and grabbed the second case of night binoculars from his cab before shutting the van doors. "Let's rock," he smiled.

"Okay?" Poppy asked Kevin.

"Ready to follow," Kevin collected Alex and moved towards his own vehicle. On either side of him, the Jersey Devil Club chattered happily and piled into Poppy's jeep and Luke and Jen's SUV. "You ready, buddy?" he asked, watching his son buckle up.

"Ya think?" he replied.

"You're a funny guy," he backed his own SUV behind Poppy's jeep. "I hear the Jersey Devil loves funny guys."

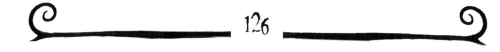

Alex frowned and looked back at him through the night specs. "I got these, dude. I'll see him first."

Kevin shook his head and followed the small caravan of vehicles onto Route 561 towards Smithville and Leeds Point. *Leeds Point*, he smiled. *The Leeds Devil.* He glanced at the clock. It was 9:35 and the road, a two lane highway in the Pines, was already empty. "Okay, dude," he said. "Then, let the hunt officially begin."

They stopped twenty minutes deeper into the Pine Barrens, down several other dark two-lane roads. Only twice, they'd actually passed houses. A handful of McMansions recently built with resettled New York money and a couple of ranches with half-a-dozen broken-down cars in the front yard. Mostly, it was the trees. With miles and miles of trees lining both sides of the road, it was hard to imagine that Philadelphia was only thirty minutes away.

The caravan took one more road, a dirt trail that ran up deeper into the state park, then pulled over. Kevin got out and retrieved his camera bag from the trunk as Alex scoped out the area.

Randy and Poppy had their night vision headsets on, the specs pushed up so they could see normally. "Everyone's communicator working?" she asked, and the group nodded back. Kevin saw that he wasn't the only one with a digital camera, and two of the college kids had brought video recorders. Short backpacks with maps, water, and ponchos were loaded on most of the backs as well.

Kevin checked his own batteries and watched the group with interest and effortless respect. These guys were taking the night, and themselves, quite seriously and in a good way. With a published zoologist and an ex-Marine leading the way, seriousness would be hard to avoid. He took several nice shots of them making their final preparations.

"Have you seen that picture of the Jersey Devil?" the one guy named Jerry asked.

"Yeah" Kevin replied. "Poppy sent me a link. Looked, well, interesting." The picture he'd seen showed only a blurred and glowing image of what looked like the chest and head of a man, a man with a very long neck and a pointed face. Odd, for certain. And, it could just have easily been labeled as an alien, angel or the *chupacabra*.

"You don't expect to take its picture tonight, do you?" Bonnie, one of the Rutgers students asked.

"We'll see." Kevin shrugged and handed Alex a knapsack to carry lighting, extra memory disks and some bottled water. He expected only to take a few nice shots of the group hunting and some eerie pictures of the moonlit pines. That's all the publisher was paying for. "If I do, I hope it's a clear picture."

"You digital?" Randy asked.

"Yeah." Kevin looked at his camera. "For about four years now. Real film's still used by some of the older guys, and for special projects, but we're almost all digital now. You know how it is. I'll get off three hundred shots tonight, easy, where real film costs me two bucks a shot whether or not the client buys. Might only take fifty pictures that way. Plus, digital grabs the light great for outdoor and night shots."

"You think that pic looked fake?" Randy pursued. "The Jersey Devil picture?"

"Getting harder to tell." He clicked another picture of Randy. "In about four minutes with Photoshop, I could put this shot of you in a dress or standing next to Britney Spears atop the Taj Mahal."

"I already got pictures like that." Randy looked over his glasses. "We ready?" he called out.

The group huddled up again quietly and methodically, but each face beamed with energy. Poppy and Jerry started forward and the rest of the group fell into a long line behind them, Alex tramping along happily somewhere in the middle. The first thing Kevin noticed was how sandy the ground was. Ten miles from the Jersey shore it made sense, but his childhood memories of camping within the unique Pines hadn't quite done this particular memory justice. It was amazing that anything could grow here, let alone the absolute forest of trees and underbrush that ran on both sides of the path. He fell back to get some shots of the group vanishing into the woods, the trees loping over them in a nice creepy frame.

They'd hiked for only about ten minutes when they came upon the cranberry bog. Some night bird made a low call from far across the dark water. "There've been several sightings in this area," Jenny reported back to him in a whisper. "We've come out here before." The water was deep and rippled towards them in the moonlight, lapping against the sphagnum-covered shore. Shadowy shapes lapped in its ripples and waves, taking form, shifting in eerie possibilities and imaginations. Patches of taller grasses and a small island in the center of the bog caused the black water to spread, making it seem like an enormous dark shape floating in the night. Kevin saw where a back corner of the bog had clearly been burnt out once by a forest fire, bare sticks reaching up towards the moon like lean, petrified fingers. He brought the camera up and took at least forty shots.

The others waited, patiently looking around the woods through their night visions glasses and shooting the sound gun in different directions. Luke had gotten down on the ground and was inspecting a track he'd found.

"What is it?" Dana asked, her voice eager.

"Just a deer, looks like," he decided. Kevin took several shots of the man crouched over the track, talking to the others. "Tracks go off that way."

"You ever find Jersey Devil tracks?" Alex asked.

"Absolutely," Jerry replied. "Well, we think. Might have just been a horse track."

"A horse with two legs?" Jenny asked.

"We took a cast," Poppy explained. "And a bunch of pictures but, they kinda vanished."

"Stolen," Randy refocused his night specs and looked out over the bog. "Ex-members."

"Ouch," Kevin offered.

"Leeds Devil evidence commonly vanishes," Dana jumped in. "Paintings, pictures, casts, whatever . . . it's part of the myth."

Convenient, Kevin thought, but kept it to himself, instead nodding politely. Poppy, it seemed, had still read the thought on his face, and her eyes narrowed some. "Let's keep moving," she suggested, and the group began its slow hike down the uneven trail again.

They came upon the old graveyard just five more minutes down the road. Most of the tombstones had been toppled over or snapped off at the base, a hundred years, or just one night of vandalism tainting a family plot more than 300 years old. He made out the name "Leeds" on several of the bone-colored stones, although underbrush had grown up into the name, half covering dates from the 1700s and 1800s. The group moved slowly about the small cemetery, taking pictures and talking quietly. It was obvious that some had already been to the gravesite but that it was new for the others. Alex stepped out of the way like a pro, and Kevin started taking shots again. He captured the group standing about the tombstones, moonlight backlighting the entire scene and then took several closeups of Jenny making charcoal rubs of each tomb. "We found this spot by accident almost a year ago," she explained. "I've been meaning to come back to get these impressions."

"And whose stone is this?" he asked her as she crouched over a simple square block that had never had a tombstone. Jenny pulled the paper back and showed it to him, the charcoal rubbing perfectly clear. "Daniel Leeds. 1741." She beamed. "Amazing."

"Maybe they were brothers," he smiled. Kevin took the picture.

"What do you think?" Poppy asked, coming up to them.

"It's perfect," Kevin said, getting up from his one-kneed position. "Better than I'd even hoped for. Thanks." She nodded and moved off with Jerry and A.J. to point out some other tombstones.

Kevin checked his watch. It was already a bit past eleven. He gathered that each of the members had come quite a way to make the outing, Johny B. up from Philley, the couple all the way from New Brunswick. It was safe to say they'd be out at least another few hours. He edged up to his son, who was busy night-scoping the various tombstones. "You're not even a little tired, are you?" he asked.

"Nope." Alex grinned, holding the specs aside. "We're staying, right?"

Kevin looked around the cemetery and took in the group. He had enough pictures to call it a night and could certainly follow the trail back to the car but . . . Alex was wide awake and having a blast. He supposed they could put in another hour and officially make it until midnight.

They started moving again, Kevin with the camera at his side so he could sit back and enjoy the outing. For the first time, though, he noticed the eeriness of the Pines. The darkness that stretched for miles, unseen and hoary limbs creaking against each other like bones. The group moved silently, following the thin trail deeper into the woods and for another fifteen minutes before stopping again. Poppy motioned him forward. "Batsto," she said, pointing. "About twenty more minutes that way, by car. Patrolled, though. And, closed."

"We could tell 'em we were lost," Luke said.

"Used that last time," Randy sighed. "Park cops get funny, you know."

"That's okay," Kevin said quickly. "I wouldn't want to get you guys in trouble."

"In that case," Poppy said, looking at the others. "Why don't we check out the area with the deer carcasses."

"Cool," Alex grinned.

"I've got a cousin who's a volunteer with the Port Republic fire department," Todd explained. "Says they found some torn up deer about two miles that way." He looked around, taking in the group. "Back at the cars in an hour," he promised.

Kevin agreed, and they started moving again. As they got closer, the group broke into natural groups of two or three and started to do a little more trail blazing. Alex asked to go with Randy; and Dana and Kevin got a nod from Randy saying it was ok. "Everybody clear?" Poppy asked into her walkie-talkie. Affirmatives came back from all, and the groups widened even more. Kevin took several shots as Alex vanished into the black woods with two of the Devil hunters, and Kevin fell in with Poppy and Johnny B.

"You don't believe, do you?" Poppy asked him as they walked.

Kevin smiled. "What makes you say that?"

"You just let your son wander off into the Pine Barrens."

Kevin grimaced. "His mother would like you." Only Johnny B. smiled, and Kevin continued. "I trust Randy and Dana. I also trust Alex. It's a group that knows what it's doing, and they're a hundred yards away. Plus, I ran around these exact same wood at night when I was eleven." His eyes roamed over the leaf-littered ground for tracks or bones, the moon dipping behind the treetops. Almost impossible to see now.

"And you weren't scared?"

"The way kids get scared, sure. Terrified one minute, joking around and completely oblivious to the Jersey Devil the next."

Poppy turned suddenly as if she'd heard something. "And what about now?"

"As a myth, I love it. I'm a Jersey Boy to the core, to a fault even, but—let's just say I'm still open to the idea of something real being out here. I want him to be out here. But, ultimately doubtful."

"That's me too," Johny B. said holding aside a branch so they could pass through. "More interested in the history of the creature, flirting with the ladies at the various historical societies and libraries. Coming out with this troop is more of a treasure hunt for me. Keeps that element of mystery and fear."

"I believe now," Poppy said. "I didn't so much when I first started a couple years ago. Then, I was just curious. But, the last year or so, I don't know. It's like he knows we're on to him or something. I get a feeling that he knows we're out here looking for him. And, while he might have kept away at first, he eventually realized we were going to stick it out. I think that's when *he* started hunting *us*."

"Hunting you?"

"Follows us sometimes. You can feel it," she said. "The eyes upon you. This extra sense of fear. Toys with us, maybe. We've heard its scream twice this year, we think. Randy lives just over in Egg Harbor City, and he swears it actually followed him home one night."

"You're kidding?"

Her face said no. "The van was scratched up pretty bad. Looked like claw marks."

"I've noticed you guys don't carry weapons."

"No way," her eyes blazed. "Two jokers showed up about a year ago with rifles and night scopes, and it was insane. The internet is great for meeting other Jersey Devil enthusiasts, but you get all sorts showing up sometimes. Perfectly normal in our chat room and then—"

"We found something." The voice came over their communicators tinny and excited.

"Where are you?" Poppy asked, dropping their conversation immediately.

Kevin suddenly caught a beam of light flashing through the forest to his right, flickering rhythmically. "Got you," she said. "Everyone else on it."

"We got him," Randy's voice came over the channel. "What'd you find, Luke?"

"Deer carcass, as promised. You guys will love this one. The thing's, um . . ."

"That's totally gross," his wife's dismayed voice came over the communicator, and Poppy grinned.

"It's kinda got no head," Luke's voice reported.

"Nice," Poppy said. "We'll be right there."

"Alex is in heaven. The headless deer will make his school report no doubt."

She turned to him. "Could be some good shots for you too, Dad."

He smiled. "Absolutely. In fact, you two move ahead. I'd like to get some from afar. Get your flashlights and video cameras glowing, forms standing within the trees . . ." He snapped several shots as the woman and older man moved towards the collecting lights.

You can feel it, he thought.

Something she'd said. A strange tingle running along Kevin's spine as if someone were standing right behind him. As a younger man, he'd worked tough shoots in Bosnia and Chechnya and well remembered the chill of fear. And, he knew he had whatever that feeling was now. Silly, he thought, and focused on the next picture, stepping closer to the gathered group. Alex and the Jersey Devil Club were only a hundred yards away.

The snap of a twig, something moving just behind him again. An animal, or maybe one of the members playing a joke. His eye counted ten forms in the lens, all bodies accounted for.

Follows us sometimes.

Kevin turned around slowly.

He took in the woods though the camera's lens, the moonlight and shadows revealing a surreal spirit world in the frame. His fingers instinctively focused on several trees, pulling in their long dark lines, the cloudy backdrop of the mysterious woods filling in behind them. And something else . . .

Another shape. He pulled his head away from the camera and took a look with his own eyes. Back in the lens, he tightened on the form again. It looked human, but there was something odd about it.

A play of light on some burnt-out tree stump. An animal of some kind.

In the lens, the thing suddenly moved towards him, creeping towards him on two legs.

Kevin fell backwards and screamed.

And took the picture.

He'd expected harassment all the way back to the trucks, but got none from the rest of the group. The club was generally concerned, and a little apologetic that he'd gotten scared, and worried themselves about what he might have seen. The pace back to the trucks was much quicker than the trip out, and by 12:50, they were ready to leave. Alex had thought it funny, of course, but was now sound asleep in the back seat.

Kevin hovered at the back of the SUV, his camera hooked up directly to the laptop for a quick review. He had to see. He'd gotten the one picture off.

The program loaded, and he flipped through the last pics, forwarding to the last shot. Picture one hundred and thirty on that disk. One more press.

Kevin Harris sighed deeply as 'Picture One Hundred and Thirty' filled in on the laptop's monitor. It showed an animal for sure. He could make out its snout and at least one eye.

"No way," he whispered. "No friggin' way."

He looked over at the others who were also packing up and climbing tiredly into the var-

ious vehicles. They're going to go nuts, he thought. It might just be a closeup of a deer, but they're gonna go nuts anyway. He looked back at the picture on the monitor.

Yup, there it was. The creature's two eyes peered directly into the camera and . . . Kevin physically stepped back from the laptop. Two eyes?

He looked at the file name again. Picture One Hundred and Thirty. That's . . . .

"You okay?" Poppy asked behind him and he turned slowly towards her voice. Her face was genuine with concern.

"Yeah, yeah," he replied vaguely. "Just, ah, checking the pictures."

"Good to follow us out?"

That's impossible. "Yeah," he said, turning towards the woods. "Yeah. Thanks again."

"Sure," she replied slowly. "You sure you're okay?"

"Yeah," he replied. "Just tired, I guess." His eyes snuck a peek at the monitor again.

"Bet you don't sleep a wink tonight," she smiled. "Just like old times."

"Right," he agreed, looking at the picture again. "You're probably right."

The picture showed its teeth now, fangs really, the head pulling back to reveal a full snarl. He thought he saw the hairy knuckles of its hand. Picture one hundred and thirty. The picture was literally changing right before his eyes, each glance another look.

"Dude."

Kevin jumped at the sound.

"Cool kid, ya got there," Randy affirmed. "He's a good hang."

"Yeah," Kevin said, turning from the monitor. "Yeah. He is."

"Checking your pics, huh? You get anything on that last one?"

Kevin looked back at the screen. In the picture, the creature's face had now turned in profile, moving away from the shot. The muzzle of a horse maybe, or the sharp curve and line of its left wing.

His trembling hand reached out and slowly lowered the laptop. "No," he replied quietly. "Nothing at all."

NOTES: There are several groups, of various sizes and degrees of organization, within New Jersey and nationally, who follow the Jersey Devil myth and also monitor current sightings as a hobby. Each weekend, one group or another may be hunting about the Pines for the elusive creature, including a state-run devil hunt held throughout the spring and summer months. The internet features hundreds of sites with information about the Leeds Devil by those who are interested in the truth behind this remarkable, and horrifying, myth and possibility.

THE WITCH'S CURSE
1735

The moon set red through the black pines. Owls hooted deep in the dark woods, and somewhere a hound howled its own ancient song to the night. The two women knelt beside the creek, candlelight flickering off their shadowed faces in a crimson glow that complemented the moonlight.

They whispered together quietly, cheerfully, as sisters do, and wrapped the thread around blackened twigs of pine and grass. The candle was passed over the sticks again, dripping over the figure and crystal beside it. Suddenly, the first woman lifted her stick figure into the moonlight and spoke out. "Water spirits return mine gift and grant good chance with every *vish*."

The other joined her, holding up her own figure briefly before laying it gently into the icy stream. It had arms and legs, a tiny straw man filled with wishes. "Let my life flow strong and pure," she recited. "A bubbling spring of joy and strength." The sticks bobbed in the stream's unhurried current as the two women held hands and recited the words again in unison. The floating figures sparkled briefly in the moonlight, then drifted slowly away into the forest's darkness.

"Thank you," the second woman said, turning.

"Do not be thanking me yet," the first replied, "Wait and see if your *vish* comes true."

Hannah Leeds stood slowly and wiped the dirt and grass from her dress. She was tall and broad shouldered, her face pale, smooth and quite beautiful by the standards of any time, framed in honey-brown hair cropped close at her shoulders. "I best be gettin' back," she said, looking to the moon. "Japhet will skin me if he finds I done sneaked off again."

The dark-haired woman looked up at her. "There are ways I can show you for that too, child." Her face was more careworn, wrinkled by sun, sea, and time. The eyes glistened like onyx. "Make him sleep plenty."

Hannah glanced at the woman, afraid of the look she might find in the gypsy's eyes. When they'd first met, she'd been scared of her. As scared as a body could be. Peggy had come off one of the fishing boats in Barnegat and spoke strangely. She dressed even odder than her speech. Hannah's own kin still whispered that Peggy Clevenger was a witch, recently escaped from Europe, and Hannah was shamed that she'd believed them at first. But, not anymore. Now, somehow, she and Peggy had become the very best of friends.

The two had met while Hannah collected sphagnum moss from the bogs, the swamp grass perfect for many ailments she came across as one of the preferred village healers and midwives. The two women spoke first only of the local plants, then simple lotions and salves. The conversation soon turned to herbal medicines, special stones, and blood letting, a common

enough treatment. They met again after that, walking through the Pines, collecting various plants together as Hannah learned of Peggy's travels in Europe and up in the Northern colonies. Eventually, they spoke of other things.

Not the kind of charms or enchantments that Hannah knew of, the folk remedies of wax and buried apple seeds that chased away bad dreams or made morning sickness go away. Peggy Clevenger spoke of another magic, conjurations of greater strength and powers older than Hannah Leeds had ever imagined.

"I wanted to show something else tonight." The dark-haired woman sighed. "Just one more."

"Not tonight," Hannah blew out her candle and collected the tiny crystal Peggy had gifted her earlier. She carefully put it into the tiny pouch against her stomach.

"The full moon," the dark woman held out her arms. "It *vill* be another month before I can show you again."

Hannah Leed's heart raced. *What enchantment would she reveal this night?* Peggy had already shown her how to start small fires with only the focus of her eyes and to get a fish to jump straight out of the stream. Enchantments revealed only at night, after the children were abed, after she'd sneaked out and crept through the brush and pines to meet her secret friend. "Very well," she laughed. "But, please hurry."

The other woman smiled and stepped away from the creek and moonlight into the dark shadow of an enormous tree. As Hannah Leeds watched, Peggy's hooded face vanished first into the darkness, leaving only the faint gleam of her eyes. Then her whole body moved into the tree's terrible shadow, and she vanished into the night as if she hadn't been standing there at all.

A rabbit emerged suddenly from the tree's shadow. It was a lean, brown hare with long ears and a short tail speckled black. It sprang towards Hannah Leeds, hopping in two great leaps to close the distance between them. Hannah Leeds gasped and stepped away, almost falling back into the stream. She laughed nervously and looked about the wood for Peggy, as the rabbit hopped easily about her feet.

She leaned closer to pick the hare up, but it jumped away and turned to watch her from a safer distance, its whiskers twitching in the moonlight. It moved suddenly and loped back into the tree's shadow.

Peggy Clevenger returned again from the darkness.

"No, that is . . ." Hannah Leeds stopped herself, then clapped her hands joyfully. "Teach me!" she cried, eyes wide. "Oh, please, show me how."

"Next full moon," the gypsy shrugged. "I can show you many things then."

"Next moon," Hannah Leeds nodded, looking up. Her hands cupped instinctively under her large belly, felt the baby growing within. In just two months, two moons, I will be a moth-

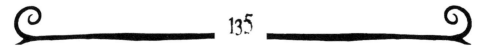

er again, she thought happily. "Soon," she beamed.

"Yes." Her new friend stepped forward and placed her own hand against the baby. "Soon," she smiled darkly.

The minister was a tall, gaunt man with tight wrinkled skin and prickly eyes. Standing at the Leeds' front step, he wore a black suit and hat, the midday sun putting a luster on his rounded forehead. There'd been talk he'd been chased from his own congregation up in Trenton and that, like a few Congregationalists before him, he'd sought a new beginning in the Pines.

Now Hannah watched him, trying to breathe normally, trying to smile.

"We have not seen you in town of late, Mother Leeds," he nodded.

"No, you have not," she replied slowly. "It be harder to get around now, Reverend. Baby's comin' soon now." She rubbed her stomach.

"Yes," He smiled politely. "God's blessing."

"Indeed," she nodded. He blinked at her, the phony smile still hanging on his face. "What brings you our way, Reverend?" she asked. She noticed that her husband hovered just behind her in the doorway, hiding in the shadows of the house. He'd taken up with the Congregationalists of late. And to drinking more lately too, much more. "It's quite a hike out here."

"Not at all, not at all," Reverend Youngman smiled widely again. "Never too far a hike to visit new congregants."

"Indeed," she said again.

"I'll tell you, though," he took off his hat. "I was thinking of your children recently."

"Were you?"

"Undeniably."

"Well, thank you, preacher. We are grateful for your thoughts." She did not keep the edge from her voice, and his smile dimmed even more. Hannah stepped out onto the lawn, gazed about the yard and tracked down four of her brood. The three youngest and an older sister played by the old white elm tree. "You have seen them at church, no doubt?"

"No doubt," he chuckled, wiping the sweat from his brow. "No doubt. Japhet brings 'em round, of course."

"Yes, he does."

He fiddled with the inside of his hat. "I'll tell you, Mrs. Leeds. There's . . . well," he

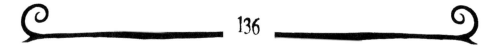

laughed. "You know how it is."

She waited.

"There's been . . . . Blessed, there's been talk about town. You and that woman."

"I see." Hannah Leeds squinted up into the midday sun, felt its warmth on her face. "Peggy Clevenger."

"She's got strange ways," the minister continued. "She's not from here."

"There's nobody from here, Reverend," she smiled thinly and looked out into the endless forest. "You're from Trenton yourself, I've heard."

"That's true enough," he chuckled again nervously. "That's true enough. The thing of it is, there's gossip now of her. Of her ways. *Unnatural* ways."

"Unnatural?" Hannah kept her voice even, steady, and tried not to laugh.

"Charms and hexes and such," he almost whispered. "She sold some kind of love potion to Sally Brickham's daughter from what I understand."

"As I cured your own sister's headaches once with feverfew," Hannah teased, smiling to ease her words. "A love charm? She's a common healer, reverend, as I am. Surely—"

"Where the devil cannot come, he will send, Mrs. Leeds. One must be careful," he warned jamming the hat back upon his head. "Especially for the children's sake. I would not want you getting caught up in anything. In any gossip that speaks of such things. Such black things."

"Such as?"

"Sorcery," he blurted meeting her eyes. "Diabolism, even!"

Hannah shot a look toward her children. *Could they hear?* She frowned. Surely not.

"A woman even associated with such dark things is endangered," Youngman cautioned in his thin voice. "A cobbler's wife I read of had been arrested for merely witnessing a witch ceremony. The name of the demon was already upon her. During the night, the devil went to her and confronted her so violently that the watchmen thought twenty horses had been let loose in the jail. When the authorities entered the locked cell the next morning, they found here dead, crumpled over, with her head awry."

Now she did stare at him. "Blessed!" she managed.

"Leviticus sayeth 'Though shalt not suffer a witch to live.'"

Hannah stepped backwards, away from him. Her head swam with sudden fear. "That is quite enough, sir! My husband will not—"

"Your husband asked me to come, Mother Leeds," Youngman stopped her, grinning suddenly like a wicked scarecrow. "He's afraid for your children. The very souls of your family."

The door opened, and Japhet Leeds stepped out onto the front stair. "It's the nightmares," he told her, shoving his hands into his pockets. He looked at her with sunken eyes. "I can't . . . I just want them to stop."

"What?" Her face crunched in confusion. "Of what do you speak? You never spoke of these things before."

"You ain't here," he snapped, lifting his head for the first time. "You off running around the woods with . . . with I don't know what."

Hannah Leeds shivered in the warm sun, standing before the two men. She would not deny the truth.

"But, I seen things," her husband waved his finger drunkenly. "At night, I see them. Strange things in my head. That—" He stopped and noticeably looked down at her pregnant body. "It's a demon," he hissed, eyes suddenly wide with horror.

"Japhet!" Hannah gasped, clutching her belly.

"I've seen it. The teeth. Oh, Lord, Hannah. It's got horns and wings. I've seen it. I've seen what it's done."

"You're not making any sense," she shrieked. Several of the other children had run up beside her, and she clung to one of her daughters. "Japhet?" she cried.

Her husband brought his arms up, covering his face, then stumbled back into the house.

Hannah Leeds turned to the preacher. "I didn't know," she cried. "What shall I do?"

"Better to keep the devil at the door than turn him out of the house," Youngman intoned. He bowed, the warning in his eyes clear as the sun as he scurried back into the pines.

They met again the next night. The red moon had dropped deeper into the forest and become a mere sliver glittering between the trees.

The dark woman sat waiting beside her hut, the old Cramer cottage, long since abandoned. She wore a dark hooded cloak, a necklace of feathers around her neck. In her hands, a single black candle burned. "What is it," she said.

"The minister come by today," Hannah Leeds blurted, half-sobbing. "I was so frightened."

Peggy Clevenger's face narrowed. "What, what did he want, I *vonder?*"

She looked up, tear-filled. "He called you a witch," she sobbed.

"Thou sayest it," Peggy mocked. "*Sortilegus. Maleficus. Venefucis. Striga.* Witch." She tittered like a child.

"He said that some women in the village were saying I was, too."

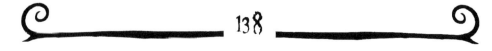

The dark woman shrugged. "Let them speak. Bad tongues and wicked ears only. You and I have grander matters to attend to. We are sisters in a higher art, a higher calling than simple gossip and superstitions. They are unavoidably jealous."

"Japhet's having dreams," she wiped the tears from her eyes. "Terrible nightmares."

"Yes, yes," the gypsy put her arm around her. "But, you already know how to make such dreams go away, *ja?*"

"Yes, I can help him."

"Good, good. Then we shall continue and deal with the gossip as we must."

"I heard they burned a . . . ." She looked up carefully. "A witch down in Mt Holly. I don't know what to do."

"Come *vith* me," the woman hissed. "There is something I want to show you." She waved Mother Leeds to follow her behind the house.

The old well rose only a few feet above the ground, crooked stones framing an uneven circle. Inside, something grumbled and spit and Mother Leeds moved closer, daring a peek.

The water boiled inside, hissing and bubbling all the way up to its very top. The gypsy woman stood over the bubbling water and waved her hands slowly over the well's opening. Hannah glanced down, her eyes widening to see the wide circle that Peggy had toed in the ground around her, a protective mark for casting. She'd stoked whatever was inside, for the sounds grew louder still. "*Bagabi laca bachabe, Lamac cahi achababe,*" she murmured. "*Karrelyos.*"

Shapes and images suddenly danced across the top of the well. The witch turned and twisted her hands in the darkness and formed the shape of a ball in the air. Something stirred within that shape. Some dark creature was curled tightly within the ball!

"*Lamac Iamec Bachalyas, Cabahagy sabal yos,*" Her words had become more of a chant and the ball dropped into the darkness beneath. Lights jumped gently across the top of the well suddenly, blue and ethereal in the night's shadows. "*Baryolas!*" The colors crept outward in the dark and danced along the rocks and trees, then across her black hood. She lifted her arms and the lights altered to violet, then swirled to red, changing, shifting. Green firefly lights, white sparks that looked like tiny sprites buzzed in long ovals above her hands, dazzling and seeming to alight on her shoulders. "*Lagoz atha cabyolas, Samac et famyolas.*"

Hannah Leeds saw the fingers then. They were long and sinewy and scaled, like the fingers of some monstrous dark jade snake. The second hand lifted over the well and both grabbed hold to pull out. She saw its sharp black claws.

Another joined the first two, lifting frothing waters below. This hand was shaggy in red-tinged fur, and much longer.

"*Harrahya!*" the gypsy cried and collapsed beside the well, hunched and crooked. The scenes that had played out across the well faded into the blackness.

139

Mother Leeds stumbled forward. "What were they?"

"Many names they have been called," the witch replied, her voice changed, deeper. "Their name is Legion, for they are many."

"They, they . . ." Hannah fought for the words.

"I have studied the *grimoires*, the black books," the odd woman explained. "And, I know how to do more than summon them. Invocation gives the means of command also. And, *with* that command comes fantastic power."

Mother Leeds glanced at the well, the bubbling within, the pops and frothing, slowing still.

"Power to fly. To turn yourself into a fox or a rabbit, perhaps. Power to injure those who have trespassed against you! The town," she hissed. "Think of the others. These, who are even now scheming against you." She placed her hand upon Leeds's shoulder. "Prosperity and well-being for your entire family," she promised. "Good food and comfort for the rest of their lives. You have only scratched the surface. This power available to so few. And, only to those who are not afraid."

Hannah Leeds trembled, breathing deeply to think through the images and warnings running through her mind. "What must I do?"

"A sacrifice, of course," Peggy replied, turning her dead black eyes on Hannah.

"What kind of sacrifice?" Hannah Leeds whispered. She'd heard such horrible stories. Stories of bones and missing children from days long past. "A goat?" she gulped.

The gypsy shook her head

"Then what?" Hannah Leeds shuddered. "What do we need?"

The dark woman reached forward and ran a skeletal finger across Mother Leeds' face. "Your baby, of course," she said. "We must have your baby."

Mother Leeds saw the black form crouched beside the shadows of the main store and fought to stay on her feet. She had not seen the woman in more than a week and had prayed earnestly to never see her again. But, as she lay awake trembling each night, she would run her fingers along the thin fresh scar across the palm of her hand, the mark of a blood oath recently made between sisters, and knew she was not yet free of the woman or the nights she'd sneaked out.

She kept walking, moving away from the thing and the dark form moved swiftly towards her.

"You sent them for me, didn't you?" the gypsy glared, suddenly beside her. "The minister

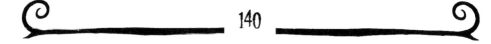

and his men."

"Go away," Hannah Leeds snarled. "I told you never to talk to me again."

The woman grabbed her arm. "They came to my cottage with their muskets and torches last night, but they couldn't find me. No," she hissed. "They couldn't find me."

"Leave me be!" Hannah shouted, pushing away.

"All they found *vas* a hare," the witch continued pressing closer. "A rabbit hopping into the woods, *ja?*"

"Leave me be," she hissed stopping. The gypsy's glare had dropped to her pregnant belly. "Leave *us* be."

"You do not understand, do you," the woman shook her head. "You have already made promises, vows that can not be broken."

"I did no such thing!" Hannah's eyes widened, her heart quailing in her chest. She shook her head, trembling furiously. She ripped the pouch from the belt at her stomach, tossing it and the crystal within at the witch. "You tricked me!"

"As you tricked your husband and children. As you trick this village still. How long before they finally learn the truth?"

"I . . ."

"Or did I dance in the moonlight alone all these many months?"

"No," Hannah allowed, wiping both angry and regretful tears from her eyes. "You did not. But, that does not mean I have become—"

"I will have this child," the woman grinned, her blackened teeth curling over her lower lip.

"No!" Hannah Leeds shrieked at the witch. She no longer cared that several men and women had stopped to watch their argument, no longer cared what the town thought about any of it. She just wanted the foul woman away from her family, her baby. "I would give this child to the Devil himself before I gave him to you!"

The witch's lips curled into a strange circular shape, the breath sucking though her teeth. The breath released again in a deep-throated laugh.

"Mercy!" another woman's voice broke through the sinister laughter, and Hannah turned slowly to the sound. "Mercy!" the woman gasped again, her face aghast. "Hannah, what did you just say?"

Hannah Leeds focused suddenly on the small crowd that had formed around them. "I . . . ."

"She cursed the baby," someone whispered.

"Leeds," another voiced confirmed.

Hannah spun, following the quickening trail of whispers, the faces around her outraged and threatening. By the time she'd looked back, the witch was gone.

Peggy Clevenger laid the first card on the table, using a hand-painted deck at least a hundred years old. The wind outside the small cabin rattled against the shutters and door, the cold winter air flickering the black candles and the lone card before her. She hunched over it, squinting.

The Ten of Wands. Force and energy applied to selfish ends, power unwisely used.

She moved from the table with the deck clutched tightly in her hand and rechecked the door. Opening it a last time, she stole a glance at the full moon again, crimson red, bleeding through the dark pines. Familiar. Outside, the black trees weaved and snarled quietly in the moon's light, an endless forest of darkness surrounded her for a hundred miles. She'd left the villages for good almost a year before and moved away from them, from Hannah Leeds and her . . . her baby. But, far enough?

She secured the door, dropping the heavy iron bar in place and shuffled slowly towards table again. The next card was drawn and laid crossways across the top of the first. *Five of Cups.* Vain regret, sorrow in those things from which pleasure was expected.

The woods had grown suddenly still, the night birds and creatures vanishing into the darkness of the Barrens. Only the flowing wind and discordant creaking branches remained. Perhaps, something else, too.

She was reminded suddenly of her travels at sea, floating still amongst the infinite lap of its dark waters, its indifferent eternal depths. The Pine Barrens has no end, she thought suddenly. Its darkness borders the very night itself and the everlasting darkness of all things. The peculiar sound outside became clearer still. The splintering of branches under heavy legs, the flutter of wings.

She shuddered, drawing the third card.

Death. The card reversed, upside down, its connotation darker still. Not the upright card of change or new opportunity, but the one of murder and oblivion.

A claw scrapped along the cottage wall. Long thick nails that trickled slowly along the length of the cabin, almost playfully.

"What?" the witch asked, clutching the deck to her chest. "What is out there?" But she knew that answer long before she'd drawn the next card.

Its breathing now joined the wind just outside, rough and deep. An excited breathing as the misshapen hand pushed through the window past her feather and bone charms, its crusted talons wrapping around the edge of the shutter.

 143

The witch placed the final card on the table, her hands beginning to shake. *The Devil.*

NOTES: The tale with the most variations is certainly how and why the Jersey Devil came to be. Some say Mother Leeds cursed the child herself, either from exasperation (The thirteenth child!) or her own dabbling in witchcraft. Another version has a young girl cursed for cavorting with a British soldier, and other popular accounts suggest that a fanatical preacher, a wandering gypsy, or the town witch whom Leeds befriended cursed the child. Perhaps, as this tale suggests, there's a little bit of truth in each. Congregationalists had settled primarily in New England during the colonial period, and they had numerous "confrontations" with witches (Salem). A small number of evangelical Congregational ministers had migrated to New Jersey and carried their concern about the occult and its dangers with them. Peggy Clevenger is the actual name of a legendary witch of the Pines, but her direct link to the Devil's birth is uncertain. She was, however, found mysteriously murdered in her burned-out cottage.